OCEANIA

AN ODYSSEY

OCEANIA

An Odyssey to the Olympic Games

The inspiring, behind-the-scenes stories of the Pacific island athletes who made the journey to train and compete at London 2012

as related by the young journalists of The Reporters' Academy

Edited by Lorna Hargreaves

uclan
University of Central Lancashire

uclanpublishing

Olympic Solidarity's aim is to organise assistance for all the National Olympic Committees (NOCs), particularly those with the greatest needs, so that they can develop their own structures to favour the expansion of sport in their country.

For most of ONOC's member National Olympic Committees, Olympic Solidarity remains the main source of income for sports development.

In 2012 Olympic Solidarity provided a special grant of US $100,000 per NOC, primarily to help with preparations for the London 2012 Olympic Games, but also to assist with other areas of priority to the NOC. For the Oceania NOCs (with the exception of Australia and New Zealand), these funds were directed towards the costs of Pre-Games Training Camps in the UK and for other preparation programs undertaken by the NOCs.

ONOC is one of the five Continental Olympic Associations recognised by the IOC. ONOC's Vision Statement 2009–12 is 'to strengthen the infrastructure of Oceania NOCs through sports development, education and cooperation with all stakeholders'. ONOC's Mission Statement 2009–12 is to 'promote Olympic values in our endeavour to assist NOCs and athletes in the pursuit of excellence at the Olympic Games.

This book has been written and compiled for ONOC by **The Reporters' Academy**: young people from TRA in Manchester and Melbourne reported upon the athletes and countries from Oceania, before and throughout the London 2012 Olympic Games. This was as a result of the Memorandum of Understanding between the North West region of England and ONOC.

Proceeds from the sales of this book will go towards the development of sport in Oceania through ONOC.

Oceania: An Odyssey to the Olympic Games

Copyright © The Reporters' Academy, 2013

The moral rights of the authors have been asserted by them in accordance with the Copyright, Designs and Patents Act 1988

First edition

First published in 2013 by
UCLan Publishing, The University of Central Lancashire
ME 316, The Media Factory, Kirkham Street, Preston PR1 2HE

British Library Cataloguing-in-Publication data
A catalogue record for this book is available from the British Library

ISBN 978-0-9565283-4-6 *hardback*
ISBN 978-0-9565283-6-0 *softback*

Designed by Lorna Hargreaves

Typeset by Carnegie Book Production, Lancaster
Printed and bound in China by Latitude Press

Thanks to all the individuals featured within this book and those who shared experiences with The Reporters' Academy crew.

Special thanks go to:

Matai Akauola	Bryan Jones
Katy Atkinson	Patrick Lawrence
Ric Blas	Mike Liptrot
Les Burwitz	Glyn McGuire
Paul Coffa	Dennis Miller
Lilly Coffa	Dr Robin Mitchell
Phil Cook	Edwina Ricci
Graham Crumb	Gareth Smith
FIVB	Debbie Wooster
Dr Neil Fowler	Debbie Jane Williams
Mary Harris	Bret Wright
Lorna Hargreaves	Rob Young
Adrian Ibbetson	Lucy Frontani (design)
Ian Irwin	Cat Bond (Oceania map)

Contents

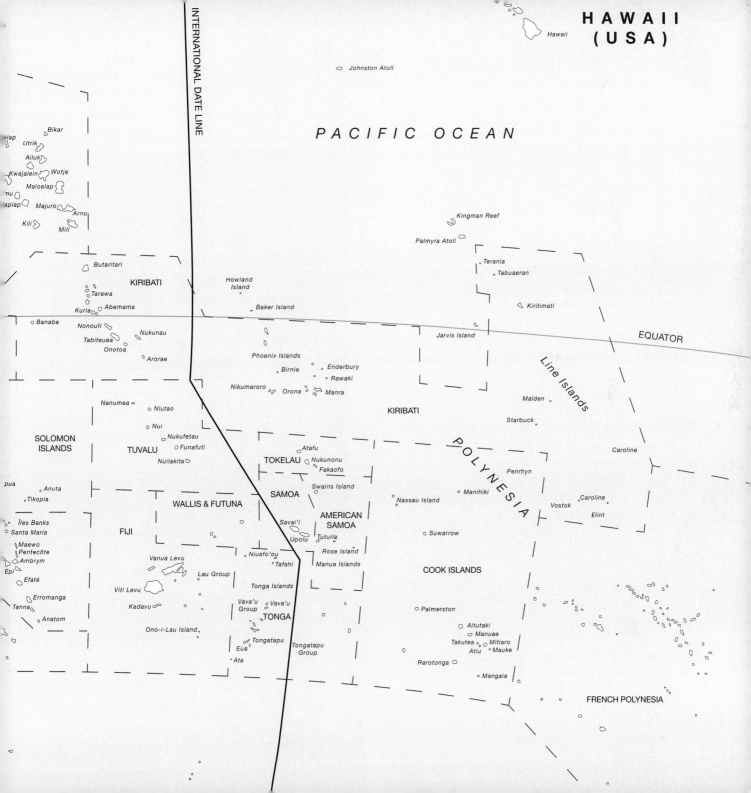

Foreword

by Dr Robin Mitchell, President of ONOC

As we begin our preparations for the Games of the XXXIst Olympiad and other international events prior to the Games in Rio de Janeiro, it is timely to reflect on our journey and to celebrate the achievements of our athletes and all those connected with them.

From my days of being an international hockey player and track and field athlete, right up to my current role as President of Oceania National Olympic Committees, I have had an abiding interest in how sport can play a central role in people's lives both culturally and socially. The Memorandum of Understanding that I signed with the North West Regional Development Agency in 2008 aimed to make a difference first and foremost to the athletes' preparations for London 2012. However, equally important was the objective of widening the participation of those in both regions, the North West and the Pacific islands.

Without doubt there can be few better examples of the successful impact of this unique partnership between fifteen nations and a UK region than is evidenced by this book. Each of the Oceania athletes made a unique journey towards London 2012, and the heart of this book resides in a sympathetic retelling of their stories. In this process, the role of several organisations in the north-west of England was crucial.

Especially fascinating are the stories behind these partnerships.

Perhaps the greatest lesson, however, is for the future: the true Olympic legacy to be glimpsed throughout this book. Through these inspirational stories, therefore, we can not only look back with fondness, but also forward with great confidence.

What better legacy than this could there possibly be?

Preface

THIS BOOK tells the individual stories of the Pacific island athletes up to and including the Olympic Games in London, 2012. They are real stories, linked by the theme of human interest. Each is told by a young journalist, a provenance that lends huge authenticity and vitality, for no jaded journalistic hack had any part in the research, interviewing or photography involved in *this* book. The young reporters had full press accreditation at the Games and were able to collect masses of unique journalistic material. Even the production and publication of the book were conducted by a postgraduate publishing student. All of these young people needed, and were afforded, support from professional mentors, industry experts and university lecturers, but this book is very much *their* work. Like the athletes of the Pacific, whose story they tell, these budding journalists and publishers have enjoyed a unique experience to be involved in what has been a remarkable odyssey.

One of the most quoted and recognisable aims of the London Games was to 'inspire a generation'. In bringing this book to fruition, the young people involved in its creation have surely helped to fulfil that aim.

How better to inspire a generation? Young dancers on London's floating Pacific island.

Introduction

B RITAIN is a very, very long way from the Pacific islands of Oceania. The two places are, quite literally, on different sides of the planet: the London Olympic Park is very close to the Prime Meridian at Greenwich; and American Samoa is almost exactly on the International Date Line, on the other side of the Earth. Farther apart would be very hard to find. The two regions are far removed, too, in terms of history, culture, economy, population density, and climate. Yet, for the last 250 years there have been close links between Britain and many of the Oceania islands. In the third quarter of the eighteenth century British maritime exploration brought Captain James Cook and others to the South Pacific, and, even today, many of the islands remain members of the British Commonwealth of Nations.

In July and August 2012, however, with the staging of the London Olympic and Paralympic Games, links between Britain and Oceania of a much more recent vintage came to fruition. For more than three and a half years Oceania athletes

'… stories which explain the athletes' long and sometimes tortuous paths in the years before they enter the stadium.'

had been taking part in Pre-Games Training Camps across the north-west of England. In doing so, they were given the opportunity to prepare for the Olympics with access to high-quality, up-to-date facilities and coaching. They were also able to forge close links with many people and organisations across the region. It is the many stories of these athletes, and these links, that are told in this book.

Appropriately, perhaps, given the prevailing climate, the deal to bring Pacific islands athletes to the North West was signed on a dull, damp,

OCEANIA: AN ODYSSEY

Above   Team Fiji arrive at the Olympic Park in London, trying to orientate themselves among the crowds of tourists.

Opposite
This is what it was all about: the London Olympic stadium, photographed in the July sunshine on the morning of the 100 m sprints.

Below   Signing of the Memorandum of Understanding, beginning the process that brought Pacific athletes to train in England's North West.

overcast day in Warrington, Friday 14 November 2008. This was the day that Dr Robin Mitchell, President of the Oceania National Olympic Committees (ONOC) and Peter Mearns, Executive Director of Marketing and Communications at the North West Development Agency (NWDA), signed a Memorandum of Understanding between Oceania and England's North West. They were joined by Olympic triple-jump gold medallist, Jonathan Edwards, board member of the London Organising Committee of the Olympic Games and Paralympic Games (LOCOG) as well as vice-chairman of their Nations and Regions Group. This memorandum enshrined a commitment for the Pacific islands of Oceania and the North West to work together exclusively on using the region as the training base for ONOC in the build-up to London 2012, and – beyond that – in preparing athletes (from those countries eligible) for the Commonwealth Youth Games in 2011 on the Isle of Man and the Commonwealth Games in Glasgow in 2014. The first group of athletes to take up training opportunities in the North West were swimmers from Palau and Fiji, who in 2009 were preparing in Liverpool prior to the world championships in Rome.

In all, fifteen island nations in the South Pacific were party to the agreement. Some, such as Fiji and Papua New Guinea, were familiar names to all of the Europeans present. But even among some of the Olympic organisers certain of the smaller states were not yet household names. At that first meeting in May 2008 most people could perhaps be forgiven for asking where exactly on the globe could one find the likes of Palau, Tuvalu, or Vanuatu? Indeed, deliverers of events and meetings over those first few months in the North West were frequently seen answering questions

Above
Nauru boxer training during their Pre-Games Training Camp in Kendal.

Below
Lord Deighton and the Mayor of Liverpool taking a keen interest in the first-ever training camp to be held in the UK ahead of London 2012.

by pointing out tiny green islands on maps of the region.

The answer was that all of the fifteen states lie in a vast expanse of the western Pacific Ocean, north-east of Australia. For sporting purposes they are all affiliated to the Oceania National Olympic Committees (ONOC). Many of the islands that are part of ONOC are independent states, some are members of the British Commonwealth, while others such as Guam and American Samoa are unincorporated territories of the United States. One island, Nauru, is the world's smallest republic, with fewer than 10,000 inhabitants on its tiny landmass of just 8 square miles. Another, Kiribati, consists of just over 30 small atolls and islands in a vast expanse of 1.3 million square miles of ocean. Papua New Guinea is by far the largest and most populous of the constituent parts of Olympic Oceania, with a population of 6.5 million. Taken together, the other 14 Oceania islands are home to another 2.45 million. The Pacific Ocean, in which they all lie, covers just under half of the Earth's water surface and about one-third of its total surface area, making it larger than all of the Earth's land area combined.

The fifteen island nations of ONOC are all relatively new to Olympic competition, with Fiji the oldest, having competed in its first Olympics in 1956. Tuvalu is the youngest, competing for the first time in Beijing, in 2008. Until London 2012 a Pacific island athlete had never won a gold medal at the Olympics or Paralympics. Only Paea Wolfgramm, a boxer from Tonga, had won an Olympic medal of any description, claiming the Super Heavyweight silver medal at the 1996 Summer Olympics in Atlanta (he was beaten in the final by current professional heavyweight champion Wladimir Klitschko). In the 2008

Challenging the next generation to a race:
Asenate from Tuvalu is photographed meeting
the local community, a useful means of
acclimatising to life and culture in the UK.

Paralympics in Beijing Francis Kampaon had won a silver for Papua New Guinea in the 100 m T46 classification. As we shall see in this book, however, that was to change in 2012, when Iliesa Delana a Paralympic high jumper from Fiji, became the first ever Olympic or Paralympic gold medallist for the Pacific islands.

From the very start ONOC's president, Dr Mitchell, was keen to link with the North West, commenting they were 'delighted to have made this long-term commitment between the North West region and Oceania, which will benefit both parties. Having visited the North West myself and seen the wonderful sports and educational facilities, I know Oceania's athletes and coaches will have the best possible preparation for London 2012.'

Such a regional approach was novel in 2012, and it prompted a unique understanding. Never before had one region agreed to provide training facilities for a group of athletes from fifteen countries, under one agreement, in preparation for a major Games. And in doing so, the agreement also helped foster links, partnerships and friendships that went well beyond mere training, and helped to inspire everyone involved with Oceania at the 2012 Games, and beyond.

For the partnership goes on. Andy Worthington, chair of the North West Steering Group for the 2012 Games, said at the time of the signing of the memorandum of understanding: 'This agreement symbolises what the Olympic Movement stands for and provides an opportunity to develop a long-lasting relationship through sport with countries on the other side of the world, while inspiring communities across the North West.' Looking back today, and reflecting on his hopes at the time, he comments, 'We began this journey over seven years ago with the message "Be Inspired". The Nations and Regions Group [for London 2012] planned to create a legacy from the outset. I believe the evidence demonstrates we've established that legacy already. However, and it is an important "however": the journey does not finish in 2012.' Indeed, it does not. Discussions are already under way to establish a UK Foundation to support education, training and sport on the Oceania islands. The universities, ONOC, Sportsworld and The Reporters' Academy are all looking to contribute and add another chapter to the story.

The north-west of England was one of the world's first industrial societies. By the end of the nineteenth century, increased leisure time for the region's coal miners and mill and factory workers had led to a huge expansion of popular participation in sports of all kinds. Each town had its football team, while many had rugby, athletics or cricket facilities, too. Today, this populous region boasts a high concentration of world-class sports facilities and infrastructure, as well as diverse regional clubs and coaches: all these assets would prove immensely valuable to the athletes who, as part of their preparations for London 2012, would be making the long journey from the South Pacific.

Toea Wisil representing Papua New Guinea in the heats of the women's 100 m at London 2012.

Javelin thrower Leslie Copeland has come a long way from Fiji. Here he is photographed mixing with other athletes during the Opening Ceremony of the London 2012 Games. Leslie briefly travelled down to London for the ceremony, but chose to return to Preston to help prepare for his event in familiar surroundings.

The North West is also notable for its warm and welcoming people. 'Wherever they [the Oceania athletes] train, I am sure they will receive a warm welcome and will thoroughly enjoy the experience.' Jonathan Edwards was perhaps not aware how prophetic his words were at the time. Not only was that true of the North West. Equally, the warmth of Oceania extended much farther than their own sun-kissed islands. The friendships, smiles and generosity of everyone associated with those fifteen nations are traits that everyone touches upon.

Wherever there are stories to tell, one needs a narrator, someone to observe and reflect upon events, characters and viewpoints, and to record them for posterity. In the case of the Oceania/North West pre-Olympic partnership, that weighty task fell to The Reporters' Academy, a not-for-profit project whose remit is to help young people expand their horizons and gain experience of journalism. Thanks to them, none of the Oceania athletes' stories was lost: indeed, all of the articles in the main body of this book are the work of those young reporters, who had unique and privileged access to the athletes and behind-the-scenes press accreditation at the Olympics themselves.

It all started quite quietly, nervously. The teenage reporters were initially faced with relatively introverted and at times sometimes shy athletes, the more so when the interviewees were confronted at close quarters with a microphone. To have travelled, as some athletes had, for the first time from their islands across the world is one thing. To discover that the media want to know their story is quite another. But such reserve was soon overcome, and Palauans Keesha Keane and Rubie Joy Gabriel, teenage swimmer and track athlete respectively, typified those Pacific traits of positive outlooks allied with cheerfulness. The teenagers of The Reporters' Academy remember meeting and interviewing their peers who were understandably nervous in front of a mic, but who continued to smile, generously give their time, and eventually become good friends with the young reporters. Over the months and years The Reporters' Academy became an integral part of the distinct coverage of the athletes from the Islands. In turn, they enjoyed and experienced a unique relationship with these teams as they built relationships which would impact upon their own lives. For instance, those teenagers from The Reporters' Academy joined the likes of Keesha and Rubie at the Games, not to watch them but to tell the world about them from the press tribunes.

The Reporters' Academy is an international sports media company whose activities provide opportunities that money cannot buy for young people between the ages of 14 and 23 to produce media, further their education, and maximise employment opportunities. Based in the hearts of two great sporting cities – Manchester and Melbourne – young people produce written, radio and video pieces across the UK and Australia. The young reporters were always on hand to document the Pre-Games Training Camps, having been given full and unique access by the various national Olympic committees, the athletes and the North West partners. This was a great opportunity to build media content around Oceania's journey to London 2012, which could be used to raise awareness across the Pacific region and, indeed, across the world.

Their work has been carefully archived, as part of that all-important ambition of Olympic 'legacy'. This book forms part of that idea.

Vanuatu's sprinter Arnold being interviewed by young members of The Reporters' Academy crew during training in Trafford.

During London 2012, ONOC suggested that the publication of a celebratory book would be one way of documenting some of the stories for future reference and audiences across the world. As a wealth of footage and text had been collated since 2008, it seemed natural to lend this to the process.

One of the advantages of working in partnership is to draw upon existing expertise and knowledge. The Reporters' Academy and the University of Central Lancashire (UCLan) had a synergy in terms of media coverage of their training camps and the shared mission of educating and advancing young people's life chances. By coincidence UCLan also has a post-graduate publishing course in its School of Journalism and Digital Communication, and this project provided one talented MA student, Lorna Hargreaves, with a unique opportunity to integrate it into their coursework, and to see the book through to publication. One of the principal criteria was that the stories are here told by The Reporters' Academy using the voices of those involved.

One of the aims of the original 2008 agreement was to develop wide-ranging links, and it is surprising just how many organisations became involved at one level or another. For example, Manchester Metropolitan University Cheshire East (MMUCE), the University of Central Lancashire (UCLan) and Edge Hill University, all based in the North West, played key roles at the heart of these stories. Not only did they provide facilities and expertise, but supported the athletes to get involved with club, coaching and competition structures in the region. All the universities provided on-site residential accommodation, along with support mechanisms such as canteen facilities, laundry, and access to social as well as sporting networks. Theirs was a professional

American Samoa's Megan Fonteno being interviewed by Dutch media, who had decided to 'adopt' American Samoa as the team upon which they would focus, reporting on their progress daily and producing short television pieces on the country and team. The production team made t-shirts showing the two flags shaking hands to symbolise their new friendship with the Pacific.

approach: like parents choosing a first school for their son or daughter, they placed the athletes in the right environments to protect and foster sporting and emotional growth.

Kendal Judo Club was one of those supportive environments. There Mike Liptrot and Ian Irwin quietly but with great effectiveness went about their work, two coaches in the sports of judo and boxing tasked with helping to enhance the Olympic chances of a number of combatants from the Islands. Ian Irwin, innovative, a master of his craft but gentle and softly spoken; Mike Liptrot, a perceptive judge of an athlete who cares passionately about their experience and guards those standards robustly. Kendal Judo Club was transformed into much more than a training centre. A dormitory was created; local visits were arranged; mobile phones bought; and the aroma of wholesome cooking frequently wafted from inside. This was the story of a community club creating a new community, of a 'wrap around' blanket which has led to further development of boxing back on the island of Nauru, supported by Ian, and a tight-knit group of judo players from across the islands, fostered by Mike. This latter group adopted the name 'Team Oceania – The Brotherhood', a reflection of the cohesion that had been created under Mike's guidance.

A great many individuals, both in the Pacific and in Britain, were involved with leading and developing the partnership. As well as the North West organisations already mentioned, there were volunteer students from the universities, administrators on each island, local physiotherapists, and coaches. At the hub of this web of activity was Rob Young, North West Coordinator for the 2012 Games. Rob not only coordinated the logistics around the Pre-Games Training Camps but also was the bridge between Oceania and the London Organising Committee for the Olympic Games. Many described him as 'the glue' that helped secure quality and delivery – in sporting terms, he was the 'go-to man'. Both Rob and Dr Mitchell of ONOC reflect in the book about the journey since November 2008, the important legacy that is being built post 2012.

Rob Young – alongside many other colleagues in the North West as well as the ever-willing secretarys-general, management and administration staff in Oceania supported and encouraged by Dr Mitchell and Executive Director Dennis Miller – was the catalyst and driving force of the partnership. Rob Young and Dennis Miller worked closely together. An important part of this book is properly devoted to their drive, originality and the impact that it had on the athletes and their journey.

For everyone the workload was high. Frequently, one could hear the phrase, 'I'm looking forward to getting home to see the family.' This could equally have come from an athlete at the end of a two-month training camp or an administrator who had been on the road for days putting logistics in place for those same athletes. Success is built upon

OCEANIA: AN ODYSSEY

Below
The final few metres of a
100 metre heat, Tuvalu and
Palauan sprinters battle it
out.

Right
Dennis Miller welcoming
Pacific athletes and
officials to London during
the Oceania flag-raising
ceremony.

hard work as well as creativity, innovation and
talent.

At LOCOG there was the National Olympic
Committees' (NOC) Relations Team who
accompanied each of the fifteen Oceania NOCs
in Oceania on the journey to the London 2012
Games. Joanna Ferris and Rob Vergouw were
particularly active championing the cause of
Oceania and acting as the conduit of information
to and from the NOCs. Both have a real passion
for the region, which has been developed over a
number of years, and this shone through no more
than when they had 'shut up shop' and reflected

on watching the Pacific athletes in action on the world's largest sporting stage from their seats in the stadia.

By 2011, a year before the Games, more countries had begun to take up training opportunities with partners in the North West. Early success of these preparations came in the qualification of Fijian javelin thrower Leslie Copeland, who had trained in the Lancashire city of Preston; the success of the Nauruan boxers at the Pacific Games in Noumea who trained in the Cumbrian town of Kendal; and the Vanuatu women's beach volleyball team, gold medallists at the Pacific Games in Noumea in September of that year. In some ways this team epitomises the whole relationship. Prior to their participation in Noumea, the Vanuatu team had trained in the somewhat unlikely setting of the workaday Cheshire railway town, Crewe, and had taken part in the beach volleyball test event in London. They even left their own little piece of the Pacific in Crewe: a beach, in the form of a volleyball training court in the town, a legacy from which the local community and MMUCE are still benefiting. Friendships and stories are now in place that will last a lifetime, and in numerous instances have been life changing. For the women of Vanuatu's beach volleyball team it will never quite be the same again. Rising hundreds of places in the world rankings, adapting to the culture of different countries and also that of their own sport. All this was achieved while managing young families thousands of miles away. The North West towns and cities of Crewe, Liverpool and Kendal were joined by Preston, Wigan and Stockport in providing facilities and an infrastructure upon which to build success towards London 2012.

This was turning into a sort of sporting and cultural family. It was as if two families had come together to be married under the roof of London 2012. For example UCLan and The Reporters' Academy continue to develop educational projects with the Oceania Sport Education Program on a range of initiatives back in Oceania to help grow sport and create a genuine sustainable legacy in the Pacific.

The scale of the partnership, and the huge distance between Oceania and the North West threw up plenty of challenges. Every participant tells tales of wrong venues, lost paperwork, deadlines missed, wrong turns taken, and language misunderstandings. Organising dozens of training camps and communicating across the world involves a panoply of logistics. All of those involved, for instance, had to take into account the different dietary customs and requirements of the athletes; knowledge of the coaching standards and how they have been training their athletes; and funding had to be secured at the right time, and in the right place. Travel, too, was challenging to organise, not only across the world but locally. Coming from a relatively small island, where transport networks are straightforward, it was not always simple to move an Olympic team, plus equipment, to Crewe from London, on a train. Just ask the Vanuatu beach volleyball team, who headed off in the wrong direction. For the universities a minibus on 24-hour stand-by became essential, and several surprise late-night airport runs had to be made.

Equally, and understandably, the athletes faced their own challenges. While the stories you are about to read celebrate this unique partnership across the world, they also give an insight into the life, hopes and challenges of elite island athletes.

Their stories provide fascinating and rarely seen insights into the behind-the-scenes world of athletes, their coaching and support teams, all striving to be at the start line of an Olympic Games. The Pacific athletes had to undertake journeys very different to those of competitors from other countries who arrived in the athletes' village in mid-July 2012. Leslie Copeland, an experienced athlete in Pacific terms, is a good example of this. The Fijian javelin thrower talks of his love of home and, despite praising the training facilities of the North West, which he acknowledges made a significant difference to his performance, he is still happy to return to his uneven practice area back on his island.

It is hardly surprising that home was a constant theme. Every islander had to travel thousands of miles just to reach Australia and New Zealand. Imagine another 24 hours' travel to the UK: it is an expensive, long and draining journey, even before beginning to put in the 'hard yards' as part of training routines. The physical distance might be measurable, tangible; however, a key element of this partnership between the North West partners and Oceania was always going to be the hidden consequences of such great distances. This was no two-week vacation of the type experienced by most of us. For the Islanders, this was leaving home, family and friends, for months on end. Some Pacific athletes and their coaches were used to this, having travelled to training camps in Australia and the United States. But for many it

was new. Also, for those stakeholders in the North West it was a learning curve in order to achieve the best possible environment to benefit those aiming for London 2012. Everyday things that we take for granted, such as communications, had to be considered. Simply, the North West's day is the Pacific's night, so contact had to be carefully organised. The planning and organization of travel, training plans, funding and medical clearance were just a few topics. Skype and email became the norm, and even on occasions this was difficult if coverage dropped out on the islands.

When the athletes arrived in the UK there were still many things to consider. Design of

BBC's Radio DJ Colin Murray and double Olympic gold-medallist James Cracknell interviewing Vanuatu's Anolyn in the Olympic Village.

training plans alongside athletes and coaches is an obvious area, but this also had to be carefully researched and thought out by the university and club training partners. Giordan Harris, the 50 m freestyle swimmer from the Republic of the Marshall Islands had spent a considerable amount of his time training in the sea at home. It was fantastic for him that he would be getting intensive training in a 50 m pool in Liverpool, but training in the sea and how that affects your swimming stroke is different to preparing for an Olympic heat in the pool. This became an important consideration for Edge Hill University and Robert Brimage, who were responsible for the swimmer's progress.

Then there were the aspects away from sport. Aspects of pastoral care had to be considered. Periods of relaxation were planned and organised. In some cases, too, help and advice had to be provided to overcome the broad cultural differences between what the athletes were accustomed to at home and what they encountered when in a country the size of the UK. Faith is important to many islanders, and access to local churches was arranged. In addition, a great deal of research was put into linking up the athletes with fellow islanders in the UK. For example, MMUCE contacted the Kiribati Tungaru Association, based in the UK, in order that they might provide cultural support for the Kiribati boxers whom the university was hosting. It was a little bit of home, which culminated in a wonderful afternoon of dance and celebration where the association's members travelled from all over England and Wales to give the boxers a send-off to a qualifying tournament in Australia.

The athletes commented frequently about the pace of life, the amount of traffic, and the sheer

OCEANIA: AN ODYSSEY

number of people in the UK compared with their own islands. In order that the athletes should feel relaxed, comfortable and safe all of their concerns in such areas had to be addressed. A lot of time was spent showing the athletes where everything was. Islanders traditionally like cooking meals with fresh, healthy ingredients, and it was a meaningful bonus when athletes want to do this. Therefore, UCLan were not the only ones to identify the best places to shop (along with the best route there, of course) for their teams in order to support their dietary requirements. This did not stop athletes from sneaking into McDonalds from time to time, as Mike Liptrot discovered with two of his judo players!

Many trips were organised to London and a range of iconic attractions in the North West, such as Old Trafford, home to Manchester United FC. All went down well, especially seeing Buckingham Palace for the first time. In cultural terms, athletes enjoyed aspects of British humour and television. A number of the athletes were fascinated by Mr Bean, the hapless TV character played by Rowan Atkinson, and expressed their interest in meeting him, having laughed at his antics on TV. Unfortunately, this could not be arranged, but imagine both the joy and the irony when none other than Mr Bean appeared, playing a significant and funny part during the Opening Ceremony of the Games.

Quite naturally, a large proportion of the stories associated with any major sporting event are about performance. Who came first? Who won which medal? What was their time? How did they perform on the day? Did they under-perform? Only rarely does the reader find out about the behind-the-scenes realities of preparing and competing at an Olympics. And that is what makes the stories

The Nauru boxers being interviewed for television while training in Kendal.

in this book so intrinsically different: for they explain the athletes' long and sometimes tortuous paths in the months and years before they enter the stadium. Every human has a story. Some are well known; some are never known. For a moment in time this book outlines a unique partnership and the legacy created out of the inspiration that is the Olympic and Paralympic Games. It tells of the challenges, barriers, successes, emotions and enjoyment through which some of the protagonists lived over a four-year period. It highlights how many people and organisations worked tirelessly to bring that original memorandum of understanding to life. It shows the passion of everyone involved to build a lasting legacy.

With the consent of his father, King Ibedul of Koror, Prince LeeBoo departeed Palau with Captain Henry Wilson and the crew of 'Antelope' to London, England on November 12, in the year of our lord 1783. While in London, Prince LeeBoo became Palau's de facto ambassador of goodwill to England and Palau's first true scholar. However, LeeBoo's plan of returning to Palau to spread universal knowledge and scientific discoveries to his people came to an abrupt end when the young prince succumbed to smallpox in the winter of 1784. The remains of Prince LeeBoo and his grand plans for Palau lie buried today in the courtyard of St Mary's church in Rotherhithe, London, England. ... This memorial is erected here, so, despite the dilapidation of time, the spirit of Prince LeeBoo shall continue to live in the hearts of the People of Palau. For a grateful nation whose spirit he invigorated and for the new generation of prolific scholars whom he inspired, the memory of Prince LeeBoo and his profound dreams, is enshrined here, now and for ever.   September 22, 1999

From the plaque on the statue of Lee Boo, in the grounds of Palau Community College in Koror

Lee Boo,
prince of Palau

'*Lee Boo is like our bridge to a different world ... it was a way for Palauans to connect to the outside world.*'

THE story of Prince Lee Boo, the young son of a Palauan chief who in the 1780s traversed the oceans aboard a small British packet ship, is now quite well known in his native land. The young prince made the journey to Britain with Captain Henry Wilson on the *Antelope* in the hope of gaining education, and establishing good relations between his island nation and the maritime superpower of the age, Great Britain. At the time London was quite accustomed to visitors from what were then considered exotic, far-away lands, and Prince Lee Boo became something of a minor celebrity during his short stay in the capital before his premature death in 1784: a few years later, in London, a short book was published entitled *The Interesting and Affecting History of Prince Lee Boo, A Native of the Pelew Islands.*

It was, indeed, an affecting story, and one which reverberates down the ages. Some 230 years after Lee Boo became the first Palaun to travel to London, a small team of athletes repeated his journey, albeit by plane rather than tiny sailing ship. The lasting historical legacy of Lee Boo travelled with them, as young Osisaing Chilton, guest of Palau National Olympic Committee's secretary-general explained: 'Lee Boo is like our bridge to a different world, I know in the past Palauans used to think we were an isolated place, but after Captain Wilson came to Palau and took Prince Lee Boo with him to London, it was a way for Palauans to connect to the outside world.' Indeed, there is plenty of evidence that the Palauan Olympic team, which consisted of athletes, weightlifters, swimmers and judokas, were inspired by the traditional story of Lee Boo, an important part of their cultural heritage, as seen particularly in the islanders' relationships with outsiders.

The Republic of Palau is a collection of 250 small tropical islands in the Micronesia area of Oceania. In the Palauan language, the islands are called 'Belau', which is believed to derive from the word for 'village', characterising the strong sense of community shared by its citizens. The islands that make up Palau have a total population of around 20,000, in other words enough to fill about one quarter of the Olympic Stadium. The structure of government has remained the same for thousands of years. Strictly speaking now a presidential republic affiliated to the United States, in fact the Palauan people are still ruled by a high chief and a royal family, much as in the days of Lee Boo's father, High Chief Ibedul.

Lee Boo's story began over two hundred years ago, when the English sailor Captain Wilson and the crew of the *Antelope* began a clandestine voyage across the Pacific from east to west. This was the time of the Fourth Anglo-Dutch War (1780–84), when Britain and the Netherlands were vying for maritime supremacy and control

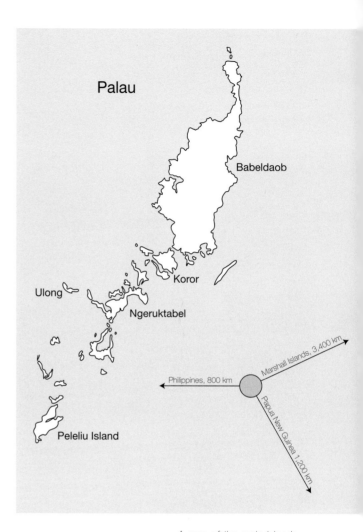

A map of the main islands of Palau. In all, there are some 250 small islands. The *Antelope* ran aground on Ulong.

over world trade routes, including to the Far East and the Spice Islands. The usual routes for British shipping westwards from China were being hampered by the ships of the Dutch East India Company. The *Antelope* had been returning from Macau by way of the Eastern Passage, a route designed to avoid the south-west monsoon, but had strayed too far east. During the stormy night of 9 August 1783 the ship was blown off course, ran aground and was badly damaged, the men shipwrecked. They took refuge on Ulong, one of the small islands of Palau.

Ulong was ruled by Chief Ibedul, who agreed to grant the men sanctuary if they assisted him in a conflict with his rival island villages. With the help of the English, who were trained and armed with modern weapons, the conflict was resolved quickly with few casualties. To show his gratitude, the high chief regularly visited and supplied the men with food while they rebuilt the *Antelope*. As a talented wood carver himself, he admired the men's craftsmanship and requested that his eldest son be taught the sailors' skills at first hand. The English stayed on the island for several months, during which time, '... from the accounts received, it was a positive relationship. We read that it was a very humane kind of treatment. The Englishmen were very kind, although they had guns and knives and muskets, they wanted to be friendly with the islanders, and the king also was kind because he was curious.' Chief Ibedul also wished for his youngest son, Prince Lee Boo, to accompany the men on their return voyage to Britain in order to learn how to be an 'Englishman'. On board the ship, the men were impressed by the islander skills that Prince Lee Boo could contribute: he was an accomplished spear-thrower and used the stars and the tides as navigational tools.

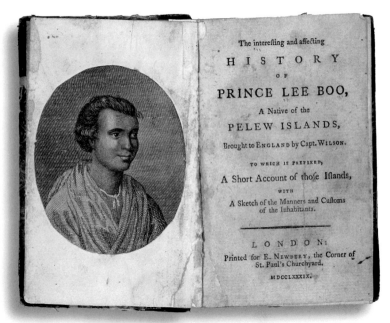

The frontispiece and title page of *The Interesting and Affecting History of Prince Lee Boo* (London, 1789). At least one book celebrating the 'moral tale' of Lee Boo was published in Paris, too.

Once in England, Lee Boo lived with Captain Wilson's family in Paradise Row, and attended a school in Rotherhithe, a seafarers' community on the south bank of the Thames in London. However, just five months after arriving in England, he succumbed to smallpox at the age of just 20. Captain Wilson is said to have called in the services of Dr James Carmichael Smyth, one of the most eminent doctors of his age, but Lee Boo died of the disease in December 1784. Before he passed away, the ship's surgeon, whom he knew well, quoted him as saying, 'Good Friend, when you go to Pelew, tell Abba Thulle that Lee Boo take much drink to make smallpox go away, but he die: that the Captain and Mother very kind – all English very good men; was much sorry he could not speak to the King (his father) the number of fine things the English had got.'

Prince Lee Boo was buried, as an 'Englishman', in the Wilson family tomb in the graveyard of the parish church of St Mary, Rotherhithe. In the graveyard there is a memorial plaque, erected by the East India Company in recognition of the kindness of Lee Boo's father to the crew of the *Antelope*, and inside the church a wooden storyboard depicts his journey to, and his experiences of, England. On the island of Koror in Palau, too, there is a memorial statue of Prince Lee Boo, attired in an Englishman's suit.

What made Lee Boo's brief sojourn in London so remarkable was that he was accepted, at least to a degree, into English society. Georgian London was one of the most cosmopolitan cities of the world, particularly down by the river, and plenty of foreign sailors and men from distant shores could be seen. Black house servants were not uncommon. Yet, for Lee Boo to be offered a place at a local school, to be educated alongside

The Wilson family tomb in Rotherhithe, London.

Englishmen, was truly remarkable. The kindness of the Palauans was repaid in kind by that shown to Lee Boo, in life and in death, by Captain Wilson.

When the Palauan Olympic team arrived in England 200 years after their ancestor, they quickly found that they could empathise with some of the experiences and feelings Prince Lee Boo must have had during his time in England. At first they were astonished by the different pace of

Rodman waving the Palaun flag in the centre of London during the Oceania flag-raising ceremony.

Live shots of Rodman on
the start line at London 2012
are shown on the stadium's
enormous screen.

life here. Just as in Lee Boo's time, London is one of the busiest places on earth; the islands of Palau certainly among the more tranquil, where a gentler pace is the norm. In addition, the ready availability of an immense variety of food types came as a shock, and in order to help the athletes adapt to living in England, and to ensure that they felt as much at home as possible, the staff at UCLan provided foods similar to their regular island diet. Further, although they resided in student accommodation, the athletes spent time with their coaches' families to assist their acclimatisation.

In the event, the Palauan athletes did not progress beyond the heats during the Games, but that would have been unexpected: the process of getting to the Olympics – and securing personal bests and national records – had been the focus of their experience. Throughout their Olympic

St Mary's church near the
Thames in Rotherhithe,
where lies the tomb of
Prince Lee Boo of Palau.

journey, the Palauan athletes were keen to
express their traditional cultural values as well as
their Olympic message. Symbolically, before the
Opening Ceremony, 100 metre sprinter Rodman
Teltull was given a blessing by the current high
chief as an act of permission to bear the Palauan
flag, and it was decided that he should don a
quintessential Englishman's suit, evoking the
memory of Prince Lee Boo and the links he had
established between Palau and the outside world
all those years before. Rodman felt particularly
privileged as this would draw attention to Prince
Lee Boo's story and demonstrate a comparison
between it and the athletes' Olympic journeys.
Rodman hopes that, through Prince Lee Boo, 'I
[will] inspire the people from Palau; the young
kids, by carrying the flag. I [hope to] make them
feel like anything is possible.'

Baklai Temengil, President of the Palau National
Olympic Committee, expressed the importance of
Prince Lee Boo's spiritual presence at the Games:
'Knowing he came to London as the High Chief's
son, it's quite a significant part of our lives. We
feel like we are home when we are in London,
because he is here too.'

After the competition, the Palauan team visited
St Mary's church in Rotherhithe, where they
were able to take time to reflect on their journey.
Rubie Joy Gabriel, a 16-year-old 100 metre sprinter
recalled: 'Similar to me, I think Prince Lee Boo
would have been scared. I think he was not used
to the weather, same as me, I was not used to

the weather when I first came to England. It was hard for me to train, because it was hard for me to breathe. The weather was really cold and I was just not used to it. I think it was strange for him when he first came here; trying to get used to everything.'

Today the story of Lee Boo is not widely known in England. Like many such stories of kindness and endeavour, the memory of it has faded. Yet, in 1892, a hundred years after Lee Boo's death, the British government did pay for the erection of a plaque to mark his burial site in St Mary's, in order, it said, 'to keep alive the memory of the humane treatment shown by the natives to the crew of the Honourable East India Company's ship, "Antelope".' In Palau the story of Prince Lee Boo's travels was only rediscovered within the last century, but it has become critical to Palauans that his story be retold in order to inspire the next generation to explore new cultures, further their knowledge, and to believe that, just like their Olympians, they can achieve anything to which they set their minds.

The story is currently taught in Palauan schools; and a set of commemorative stamps has been issued, with illustrations of the prince, the *Antelope*, and the East India Docks in London. Likewise, the Palauan National Olympic Committee hopes that these Olympic values will continue to resonate in Palau.

Baklai Temengil has expressed: 'This is not really the end of it, it's just the beginning of inspiring, continuing to have that energy, the synergy from our leadership, the community of Palau, it's real, it's really making an impact on our young people's lives and we have to continue to inspire and maintain and having more people aware of that, it's a life-long experience.'

Young competitors Keesha Keane (from Palau) and Ann-Marie Hepler (Marshall Islands) in Liverpool training for London 2012.

Inspiring a
new generation

I IN Singapore in 2005, when the world heard the news that London had won the bid to host the 2012 Games, Sebastian Coe proclaimed to the world this Olympic message: 'Today, London is ready to join you in facing a new challenge and to provide another enduring sporting legacy. Today's challenge is tough. It's more complex. We can no longer take it for granted that young people will choose sport. Some may lack the facilities. Or the coaches and role models to teach them. Others, in an age of 24-hour entertainment and instant fame, may simply lack the desire. We are determined that a London Games will address that challenge. So London's vision is to reach young people all around the world; to connect them with the inspirational power of the Games.'

From the start young people were to take centre stage. In Britain one youngster was already having to get used to fame: Tom Daley, British junior champion diver, then aged just 11, became one of the faces of London 2012. His picture was splashed all over the media and even adorned some of the

'London's vision is to reach young people all around the world; to connect them with the inspirational power of the Games.'

Young Olympians from Guam, Mashall Islands, Fiji, the Federated States of Micronesia, Palau and American Samoa are photographed alongside some of the young Reporters' Academy crew who helped tell their stories.

city's iconic red buses. By the Beijing Games in 2008, Tom was already an established elite athlete, even though he had not yet reached the age of 15. In 2009 he became world 10 metre champion, and he was still just 18 when he competed in 2012.

Twelve thousand miles away the sporting journey of another young athlete, Palauan swimmer Keesha Keane, was starting upon a similar, if less well publicised, trajectory. Keesha is a 50 metre freestyler. At the age of 15 she became the first female Palauan swimmer to achieve a time of under 30 seconds: 29.99 at the Guam Championships a year before the Olympics. She was still just 16 when she competed in the London 2012 Games.

Another Palauan competitor, Rubie Joy Gabriel, is a runner who competed in the prestigious sprinting distance, the 100 metres. Unlike Britain, Palau does not have an advanced social media network and it is difficult for the girls' friends and family to keep in touch with their progress. However, the girls had the support of Palauan TV. Keesha, has appeared on Oceania Television, as she explained: 'Before and after the Olympics I had a couple of interviews from the media here in Palau, asking how I felt and if I was scared or excited. Even after they announced it and everyone saw me on TV I went to school and some of my friends would tell me they saw me on TV and that's so cool that I'm going to the Olympics. My relatives were so proud and surprised that I'm going at such a young age. Even at this time still, strangers say "Hi" to me and I don't even know their names and they would be, like, "You're that swimmer right?" It's pretty cool. Now the question everyone's asking me is that if I'm going to the next Olympics. I don't really know what to say yet.'

The girls' island home is very different to that of Britain's young diving star: Palau has a population of 21,000, which is one-tenth of that of Plymouth where Tom Daley was born. One of the main talking points around Daley was how he would handle all of the media attention. In fact, in the UK, people in his position are offered training in how to deal with the press. In contrast, Keesha and Rubie struggled to gain publicity because of the limited social network in their country.

Indeed, journeying to the UK was the girls' first time away from home. Keesha explained some of the differences she noticed while training in Britain: 'The major difference were the facilities.

Oceania swimmers connecting with the local community of Liverpool.

Team Oceania dominating the track during the heats of the women's 100 metres. Rubie Gabriel (Palau), Pauline Kwalea (Solomon Islands), and Patricia Taea (Cook Islands).

The pool was larger, more swimmers, a gym right around the corner, and the lockers were huge. Back home we swim outdoors. It's mostly hot so it doesn't feel good. We don't have the best starting blocks as well, so at least the blocks in Liverpool were similar to the ones in the competition, which helped me get used to the real blocks.'

When you meet them Keesha and Rubie come across as typical teenagers: fun, excitable, and full of energy. But they also share a mental maturity, which is an asset to their training and

OCEANIA: AN ODYSSEY

Below
Team Tonga inspiring the
next UK generation.

ambition to progress as far as they can. Preparing for a major Games at such a young age tends to build a mature and characterful attitude to life, competition and training.

Keesha's passion for swimming began when she was young. Her parents encouraged her to attend swimming lessons and to go away to camp where she quickly discovered just how good she was at the sport. While training in Liverpool, both girls focused on achieving their personal-best times: Keesha was determined to swim in under 26 seconds, while Rubie was aiming to run below 13.48 seconds for her 100 metre race. During this time of preparation the two girls developed a close bond. They certainly needed each other's support, for while they were excited to be part of the Olympics and demonstrated a fearless approach to their journey, they found it difficult to be apart from their families. Keesha recalled: 'I am used to being away from my family but I always miss them. Before I came here my grandmother gave me a little gift which I carry around with me. It gives me luck and it reminds me of home.' She also missed not being 'able to hang out with her friends', but appreciated 'the unique opportunity I had to visit many countries, and my friends understand how lucky I really am'.

So how did all the young competitors get on? In all, 9 of the 13 athletes from the Oceania region who were 18 or under, achieved a personal best. Rubie was no exception, running a personal record in her heat (13.34 secs) in front of 80,000 spectators; Tom Daley picked up a well-deserved bronze medal, and Keesha stood proudly at the poolside, waving joyously at her parents as a thank you, having finished a highly respectable fourth in her heat. She, too, achieved a personal best, of 28.25 seconds for her 50 m event at London 2012. Keesha admitted to her ultimate ambition: 'I hope to be the first Palauan to win an Olympic medal.'

Keesha and Rubie are role models for other young competitors, to aspiring young athletes and to the people of Palau. Their Olympic aim is 'to teach young ones and to inspire more young ones to attend swimming and athletics clubs'.

Anthony (judo) and Nathaniel (wrestling) of American Samoa, wearing their traditional outfits for the Opening Ceremony.

The Opening Ceremony of London 2012

A POTPOURRI of British culture, created by the mind of Danny Boyle, director of the award-winning film *Slumdog Millionaire*, welcomed 204 international teams from around the globe for the opening of the 30th Olympiad. The opening ceremony at London 2012 was a very British affair, highlighting the country's industrial history, its varied culture and music, and its sense of humour, including guest appearances by comedian Rowan Atkinson on keyboards, and a dramatic entrance by the Queen accompanied by her very own special agent, James Bond, 007.

In a very similar way, for each of the 15 Pacific island communities competing under the umbrella of Oceania this was the perfect opportunity to introduce and display their pride and cultural heritage to the world. The competitors from all of the Pacific communities represented at the Olympics seized that opportunity, beginning with the American Samoan swimmer Ching Maou Wei, who was the first flag-bearing athlete to represent the Pacific islands.

OCEANIA: AN ODYSSEY

He explained: 'Every part of our costume has a meaning, and is a real part of our traditions. My team mates Nathaniel Tuamoheloa [who competed in the wrestling events] and Anthony Liu [a judoka] were dressed as "Matais", leading the team out into the ceremony, acting in the traditional role as chiefs.' Fa'amatai is the name given to the indigenous governmental structure in American Samoa and the Independent State of Samoa which are ruled by a high chief. The prefix *fa'a* is Samoan for 'in the way of', and *matai* means 'family name or title'. Looking after their people, like a 'family', is central to the high chief's role. This Samoan team felt very much like a family, proudly taking their place on the world's stage.

For the occasion Nathaniel and Anthony wore the 'Le Faitage', a single rectangular cloth worn as a skirt – an article of everyday clothing for Polynesians and other Oceanic peoples, with the 'fue', an item of regalia traditionally worn by a Samoan Tulafale (or 'talking chief') on their shoulder and held a staff called a To'oto'o (used by a high chief when making speeches in the open). Anthony recalled that, 'as I entered the stadium it felt as if the energy came from within; everyone was cheering for us.'

Ching explains that, 'I was in awe, taking in the moment. I was so happy and excited, such a mix of emotions. My favourite part was the lighting of the Olympic torch. The design was so artistic, and best of all, it kept me warm as it was a cold night for us compared with home!'

'As I entered the stadium it felt as if the energy came from within; everyone was cheering for us.'

The parade of athletes: Guam, American Samoa, Fiji, and the Cook Islands. How the Olympic torch would be lit was a closely guarded secret. When more than 200 copper petals – each representing a country, and carried into the stadium by the team – were lit, coming together to blossom into a flower that would burn brightly for the duration of the Games, the effect was magnificent. All the National Olympic Committees around the world have now been given their original petal, a perfect memento and reminder of the significance of the Olympic flame.

The view from the press seats, which were occupied by the young crew members from The Reporters' Academy, fully accredited reporters for Oceania.

THE OPENING CEREMONY

Tuvalu fly their flag in front of the millions of people around the world who tuned in to watch the Opening Ceremony. The flag is borne aloft by weightlifter Lapua Lapua.

Nathaniel Tuamoheloa, who represented American Samoa in the +93 kg wrestling, added: 'Everyone wanted to take pictures of us, and it was great to see that many people watching me and the team.'

Such emotions were echoed by 50 metre swimmer Giordan Harris from the Marshall Islands: 'I'm from a very small island in the Marshall Islands, it's only one mile long. Being raised there all my life, I've never seen anything like the opening ceremony. It was absolutely amazing.'

For Marshallese sprinter Haley Nemra, by contrast, this was her second Olympic Games: 'Some of my friends told me there was going to be four billion people watching, and it was just incredible, I tried not to think about all the people watching me, so I just had to smile and keep going.'

While waiting behind the scenes, with Team Tonga, before joining the ceremony, Alison Donnan remembers that she 'was overcome with excitement. As the team physiotherapist, being involved in the world's most elite sporting event was incredible. I felt enormous pride standing next to such great Tongan athletes. The U2 song 'It's a Beautiful Day' was playing … and indeed so it was.'

The Secretary General of the Tonga National Olympic Committee, Takitoa Taumoepeau, spoke of the pride he felt being involved with London 2012: 'The Olympic Games are the pinnacle of multi-sport events, a dream for athletes and officials to be part of. To be there was exceptional, especially for me as I was joined by my wife and daughter. It was a wonderful time for family and for sporting reasons, due to the history of the host nation and the city of London. Tonga has come a long way; taking part is winning for us, especially when thinking of all the hard work and preparation behind the scenes by our National Federations and our National Olympic Committee as a whole.'

As a first-time secretary general of Team Fiji, Lorraine Mar, said, 'it couldn't have been a prouder moment for me. For the lucky members of Team Fiji who marched around the Olympic Stadium, I'm sure it was an experience of a lifetime and one that they will cherish for ever. For the minutes that it took to complete the 400 m parade around the track, they were proud to be promoting their country to the world. Going into the Games, our aspirations for our athletes were that they compete well and deliver their best performances. London 2012 saw four Fijian athletes qualify for the Games on merit – the highest ever number of Fiji athletes to qualify for an Olympic Games.'

Contrasting with Danny Boyle's journey through the greyness of the industrial history of the United Kingdom, the colourful extravaganza provided by the athletes of Oceania brought to the international stage an insight into another, more exotic, world.

As an engaging means of raising awareness about the region and its wonderful culture, members of the Pacific community perform a traditional Fijian hand dance on the floating pontoon in St Katharine Docks, London.

A Pacific island in the heart of London

O N the evening of 30 July 2012, three days after Danny Boyle's opening ceremony had exhibited his vision of British culture to commence the 30th Olympiad, a corresponding vision of the Pacific islands was brought to life aboard a floating pontoon in one of London's historic docks. St Katharine's Dock was built in the early years of the nineteenth century and for decades welcomed merchant sailing ships from around the known world, laden with foreign goods and crewed by sailors of many tongues. The dock is built right next to the famous Tower of London, just outside the eastern boundary of the ancient City of London; this was a highly visible and accessible location for visitors, tourists and Londoners.

Throughout the period of the Games the pontoon welcomed around 10,000 guests and passers-by to enjoy a spectacle of traditional dances, singing, food and entertainment, showcasing Pacific culture and heritage. On this particular evening, 30 July, the festivities were

photographed and recorded for posterity. It was a
truly memorable evocation of the Islands, a Pacific
island right in the heart of London.

ONOC's President Dr Robin Mitchell explained
the aims of the performance: 'We come to an
Olympics to make our mark in different ways. We
are a few years off athletic excellence so we have
brought our Pacific communities living in London
together to provide a cultural and social program.
Unless we are working together to support each
other we can't make that difference.'

On this particular night The South Pacific
Tourism Organization, The Oceania National
Olympic Committees and athletes and coaches
from American Samoa, Fiji, Papua New Guinea
and Vanuatu, were all in attendance and eager
to take part. Yoshua Shing, an athlete from
the Vanuatu table-tennis team, expressed his
enjoyment at seeing all of his fellow athletes: 'In
the Commonwealth Games and Olympic Games,
all the Pacific islanders, we are like a big family
and I'm really happy to see them there.'

Jane West, who was representing Tourism Fiji
UK, explained the importance of the pontoon from
her perspective: 'The fact that the Pacific islands
had a high profile "floating" national house during
the Olympics was a major breakthrough. From a
tourism perspective it was a unique opportunity
for Tourism Fiji. Sports and tourism complement
one another and this was an occasion to bring
Oceania's athletes, the Pacific communities in
London, the public and the travel industry together

OCEANIA: AN ODYSSEY

Upper   Traditional Fijian patterns can be seen on the outfits. Masi cloth, a traditional bark-cloth made from the paper mulberry tree, is used. A sea-shell necklace is also worn.

Lower   A group of energetic traditional dancers share their moves with the visitors at St Katharine Docks. They sport traditional face paints and grassy arm bands.

at a time when the public's interest in the Pacific was heightened.'

In Fiji's case the night began with a traditional dance, performed under a wooden canopy, by two elder women and two younger girls, from the host country, who were dressed in richly coloured sarongs. This was followed by another performance, and one that turned out to be a real crowd pleaser; a group of men from Fiji, wearing grass skirts with black paint on their faces, created a hectic tribal dance. The leader of the group began with a solo performance before being joined by two teenagers and three younger boys who danced in synergy with him.

There were strong messages in some of the performances that night, notably from a group of Papua New Guinean women who performed a dance that expressed their pride in their female form.

As the evening progressed and the temperature began to fall, Sani Muliaumaseali'I, a singer from Samoa, kept the crowd in high spirits by making them laugh and encouraging them to sing with him: 'Louder!' he energetically cheered, 'then you'll be warmer! In the islands we like to sing *together*. For me to come by myself is a bit strange, very strange,' he told the audience. He was not to be disappointed.

To finish off the night, a Fijian man dressed in traditional clothing and carrying a flaming torch led people off the pontoon and up the ramp to a restaurant where there was a chance for the

A group of Pacific women, showing traditional outfits that may be worn by all ages.

Samoan singer Sani Muliaumaseali'i entertains the crowds. 'Louder!' he cheered energetically, 'then you'll be warmer!' He is seen here with a Pacific chief fly-whisk, now a decorative object, but traditionally used to keep flies from bothering the high chiefs.

athletes, dancers, officials, media and the general public to become acquainted and socialise.

The High Commissioner of Papua New Guinea in London, Winnie Kiap, was delighted with the evening and enthusiastic to keep working with Oceania countries: 'One of the very important aspects of any games is to build peace … for myself, [what] I value most is the fact that people are coming together, enjoying being together, respecting each other for their excellence, for what they are good at and this is the way that peace is built.'

A PACIFIC ISLAND IN THE HEART OF LONDON

American Samoan swimmer
Ching Maou Wei stands by the
blocks, preparing to compete in
the heats of the 50 m freestyle.

High emotion amid stirring achievement

'I will definitely go down in history, so that's a legacy in itself from the London Olympics.'

Ching Maou Wei, 50 m freestyle

On 2 August, Ching Maou Wei, from American Samoa, swam the 50 m freestyle. Ching was drawn in Lane 3 Heat 2, and was raring to go and start his competition. At the moment when Ching hit the water his Olympic dream began.

As soon as he entered the arena for his qualifying heat he was greeted by an applauding, enthusiastic audience. Sporting his country's dark blue tracksuit, he felt encouraged yet nervous by the enormity of the crowd and their support: 'I kind of had a couple of butterflies going on, but was focused on my race.'

He was able to remain composed and take the experience in his stride: 'I knew I wanted to get quick off the block and go quicker.' Among the flags, flashing cameras and cheering faces were a small group of fluttering American Samoan flags, waved enthusiastically by other team members.

'It gives you a boost of confidence, knowing that team mates are out there cheering you on.'

London 2012

Left   Ching catches his breath and looks back at the results board to assess how well he raced.

Above   A view across the pool. Ching is in the third lane in Heat 2 on 2 August 2012.

Ching goes through every moment of that second heat, almost like a check list: 'quick off the block ... wasn't too good today ... feel like I could have been faster ... especially off the blocks ... felt like I could have got a better time.'

Despite this, he in fact touched home in a time of 27.30, a new personal best for the American Samoan swimmer. Ching finished third in his heat and 51st overall and can take a lot of fond memories, as well as his new personal best, away from his first Olympics.

OCEANIA: AN ODYSSEY

Robert Vergouw, NOC Relations Team

If anyone appreciates the scale of the challenges faced by the Pacific islanders in qualifying for and competing in a major Games it is Robert Vergouw, who, as the National Olympic Committee Regional Coordinator, worked with LOCOG and helped ensure that all the athletes from the 15 Oceania nations got to the Games fit, well, and ready. Working closely with the athletes, he is well placed to describe the emotional highs and lows of their personal journeys. For example, of Manuel Minginfel, a weightlifter from the Federated States of Micronesia (FSM), with whom he had worked very closely: 'Manuel captivates the audience with his raw energy, and his presence on the field of play is something that you cannot help but admire. He is as elite as an athlete can get. When he walks out for his lift and the crowd falls silent you cannot help but support him, you get caught up in the emotion that he shows. It's the tiny nation of FSM on the world stage and you can feel that Manuel is lifting for his home. Every lift gets a gold-medal winning reaction from him. I felt proud that Manuel was on the world stage gaining respect both for himself and his home country and showing that they deserve their place on this stage.'

'These are some of the most isolated nations competing in the Games so even travel costs almost become prohibitive in getting athletes flown around the world to compete at World Championships, World Cups and other qualification events.'

American Samoan sprinter Elama Fa'atonu also made a lasting impression on Robert. He was the first Oceania athlete to arrive in the Athletes' Village and, to make him feel welcome, Robert asked him about his journey to the Olympics, whereupon Elama explained that he had been away from his family for a long time and that he missed them desperately. Robert then began helping him to telephone his mother and speak to the rest of his family. Speaking to athletes such as Elama helped Robert really come to terms with what the athletes from Oceania had been going through and the sacrifices they had made to get to the Olympics: 'This really put the athlete's experience into perspective for me. Then being able to see him compete in the Athletics 100 m in the stadium in front of 80,000 people and speaking to him after it … this, to me, was an insight into how it would have felt, how it made him feel, and the significance of it for him.'

Robert concluded: 'To see athletes from the 15 islands I worked alongside, such as the Cook Islands, Vanuatu and Papua New Guinea, compete at the pinnacle of their sport is truly inspiring. These elite athletes are representing their countries and are their nation's best athletes, doing something that only a small percentage of the world are privileged ever to do. Just being around this fills you with a tiny fraction of what they must be feeling and it makes you sit back in awe, and you cannot help but get caught up in the moment and cheer like crazy.'

Elama preparing himself on the start line of his 100 m sprint. Among the 80,000 crowds was Rob Vergouw, watching on nervously.

Above   The flag-bedecked headquarters of the NOC Relations Team at the heart of the Olympic village. This is where Rob's team cared for the 15 countries' every need.

Below   Elama in action racing alongside John Howard from FSM and Chris Meke Walasi from the Solomon Islands.

Above   The moment when Oceania NOC administrators from Nauru and the Solomon Islands met Her Majesty the Queen, representing their countries proudly.

Below   Pacific island swimmers enjoy a much-needed period of relaxation.

The Vanuatu beach volleyball
team – Joyce Joshua, Miller Elwin,
Henriette Latika and Linline Matauatu
– photographed on their island.

The emergence of Vanuatu's beach volleyball women

The team practising at home in Vanuatu.

I N terms of sporting development and improvement in performance, few athletes from the Pacific can compare with one group of four young women from Vanuatu: the island nation's beach volleyball team. Within just a few short years before London 2012 their performances improved enormously, their world ranking soared, and their status both in their home island and in the beach volleyball community was utterly transformed. From obscurity the island team now competes at the highest level around the world.

Situated off the coast of northern Australia, the islands collectively known as Vanuatu have a population of approximately 256,000. Its warm climate and tropical topography, its white sandy beaches, rainforests, mountains and clear waters, all tend to obscure the realities of an economy that is struggling to meet the demands of its growing population.

In 2006 Vanuatu held a competition to find sportswomen who could become part of a national beach volleyball team for the 2012 Olympics.

Opposite
Vanuatu's Henriette Latika
defending against Australia's
Taliqua Clancy in Thailand.

Members of the team at home in Vanuatu practising and relaxing. While at home the girls chose to wear casual clothing rather than the bikinis that are *de rigueur* in competition.

Miller, Linline and coach
Lauren in Crewe at the
Pre-Games Training Camp.

The whole team photographed on Vanuatu. The island is
still well wooded, although under pressure from increasing
population and deforestation.

terms of their social and cultural values, their language and their means of communication. Teaching and coaching methods had to be altered promptly: 'I had to adopt different ways of coaching, different ways of communicating, using a different methodology and very simple visual and kinaesthetics rather than just being able to say things in words and have it immediately understood.'

Lauren commented on one particular cultural difference, which affected the most fundamental forms of interaction: 'Ni Vanuatu don't tend to look people in the eye, as it can be considered offensive, aggressive or rude. In our society, on the other hand, it is considered polite to look at someone when they are speaking to you. All of this can cause great confusion and even frustration. I also had to endure long silences as they are quite comfortable not responding to questions immediately or even in a close time frame.'

Lauren found that one of the biggest challenges when working with the team was their reluctance to wear the conventional form of attire for the sport: 'There were obvious cultural differences in what is considered appropriate attire for women, which did not include the standard dress uniform, the bikini. There have been many challenging situations involving partners and the general community back home to accept the bikini as a playing-uniform requirement. We had to allow the girls to train in more conservative attire whenever they were on the island.'

During the time Lauren spent with them, however, the women did gradually become more inclined to wear the bikini when practising and competing away from home: 'At the first training session we had in Australia, the girls were wearing oversized t-shirts and tights; then we had to train them into downsizing their uniform sizes over the course of the training block so that when we arrived on our first World Tour the girls were

OCEANIA: AN ODYSSEY

semi-comfortable to wear the briefs. We started in tights, and shorts, moved to long leg bike pants, then on to massive bloomer-style bathers, then finally into normal bikinis. Amazingly, all the girls played in New Zealand last year [2012] wearing Brazilian brief style bikinis. Oh how far we have come! Alas, on the island, the team was still wearing t-shirts and shorts, but we wanted to uphold the values of the country and so the girls still have the right to train and compete on the island in whatever clothes they choose.'

When the Memorandum of Understanding was signed in 2008, it was decided that to prepare for the Games the Vanuatu athletes should be based at Manchester Metropolitan University Cheshire East (MMUCE) from 2010. Here they would receive fitness and sports-medicine assessments and advice. During this time, the students of the university introduced the team to the community of Manchester to help them to acculturate in preparation for the Games and improve their knowledge of British culture as a whole. In addition, the athletes received media training.

Days before the team's arrival in Manchester, in 2010, however, MMUCE realised that they quickly had to address one rather crucial issue: the absence of any beach volleyball court in Cheshire. A temporary facility was established on a former ménage at a farm, which was owned by the father of a technician who worked at the university. A year later this was replaced by a permanent court on the MMUCE campus where the team notably

benefited from the assistance of professionals, administrators, physiotherapists and sports scientists. This was particularly helpful because, in 2011, they were invited to participate in the Olympic test event at the real Olympic venue of Horse Guards Parade in London. As their presence in the UK excited interest, their progress received media coverage in British national and regional newspapers, and they appeared on British news and featured in a documentary.

In 2010 the team competed in another FIVB World Tour event, this time visiting London,

Finland, Norway, the Netherlands and China. As it transpired, 2010 was a year of great progress and confidence building. In that year the Vanuatu team held their first training camp at MMUCE, and in the China World Tour event they won a very notable gold medal. This was a major breakthrough for the team, which helped to generate publicity and increase public support at home.

Their confidence had also grown as they toured and accumulated experience of playing at a competitive level and experienced other cultures.

Food presented a challenge to Lauren as the girls developed a liking for different international cuisines. At the time, Lauren remarked: 'a few of the girls now can even use chopsticks very effectively.' They also acquired experience of public speaking as ambassadors and professional sportswomen of Vanuatu.

However, it would be wrong to suggest that success came easily to these women. At every stage their journey to the Olympics was challenging. The first hurdle to overcome was

Opposite   The team taking part at international level, now comfortable playing in their bikinis during competition. Top left: blocking the ball against the Brazilian team while competing in Brazil; top right: Joyce Joshua (left) and Linline Matauatu; bottom left: Joyce Joshua diving for a shot in Brazil; bottom right: Henriette Latika dives for the ball watched by her partner Miller Elwin.

Below   The girls showing how it's done, on a farmer's specially built temporary court in Crewe.

Competing at international level allows the girls to travel afar: the upper photograph captures them in Thailand, the lower in Brazil.

started the FIVB World Tour in 2010 they were ranked 350th, and this had risen to an incredible 29th prior to the London Olympic Games. The team had risen 314 places in the rankings in just three years and never lost sight of their Olympic goal. They failed to qualify for London 2012 by such a small margin – by losing the final of the Asia Continental Cup to China (who eventually came fourth in London) – but their results since then confirm that the attitude of the team is still incredibly positive. They have now broken into the FIVB world top ten, finishing ninth in Thailand and then achieving a silver medal at the Asian Championships, losing out only to China who are currently ranked second in the world. Finally, in 2012 they beat Australia to win gold in the final of the Oceania Championship and were awarded the Pacific Team of the Year by the Pacific Games Council.

The growth in confidence of the players has been phenomenal, and they developed the ability to perform consistently despite the lack of physical resources, scientific support systems and, crucially, funding comparable to that of the top teams. Indeed, their hopes of competing at the next Olympics are still dependent on finding a secure source of funding.

Of equal importance is the legacy on the Pacific islands of the team's overall performance in the years leading up to 2012. The effect on the aspirations, attitude and positive behaviour of young Vanuatu and Pacific islander athletes, especially the young girls, will surely last a lifetime.

Back home in Vanuatu, a transformation was already taking place, offering new hope for the cultural advancement of women in society. A youth programme has been organised to encourage young women's interest in beach volleyball. Even today, however, the team's funding remains precarious and slight, although the use of social media has helped with raising their profile, and has provided them with further sponsorship prospects.

The women are very proud of what they have achieved. They have become inspirational role models, not just for the youth of their country. They have also given hope and inspiration to many athletes and women throughout Oceania. They have proved to themselves, to the world and to their country that they are strong and successful women.

The MMUCE training camp has established relationships which will act as the bedrock for further developments regarding Pacific training camps for future events such as the Commonwealth Games and even Rio 2016.

So now their journey begins again as they endeavour to become one of the only Pacific island teams to qualify for the Olympics purely on merit.

The team photographed back on Vanuatu after London 2012, relaxing on the beach and looking forward to future events and challenges.

Upper Iliesa Delana was accorded a military parade, and he inspected a guard of honour. Here crowds welcome him into the Vodafone Arena, where he and his coach were received by the President Ratu Epeli Nailatikau and the First Lady, Adi Koila Nailatikau.

Lower The ceremonies to honour Delana's achievement took place inside the Arena. Here the President hands Delana a gift from the Government of Fiji.

Upper A homemade banner showing the moment when Iliesa won his gold medal. A young disabled fan is seen admiring his hero: what a fine role model to the youth of the Pacific. The Fijian fans are wearing their colourful outfits on this day of celebration.

Lower Homemade banner and balloons. This photograph shows some of the hundreds of people on the celebration march through the city of Suva, many of whom took time off work in order to take part.

Iliesa Delana: first ever gold for the Pacific islands

Iliesa Delana. (All photographs by Fijian journalist Matai Akauloa.)

T WENTY-EIGHT-YEAR-OLD Fijian athlete Iliesa Delana is a true example of sporting inspiration. At London 2012, in his final high-jump, he cleared 1.74 metres, a personal best and an Oceania record. What makes this all the more remarkable is that when he was just three years old he had survived a serious bus accident in which he lost one of his legs. Among Oceania's Paralympians, he towers above all others.

In 2006, when he was twenty-one, Iliesa competed in a one-legged high-jump event in The Far East and South Pacific Games for the Disabled. The Games are one of the biggest multi-sport events in Asia and the South Pacific, and it was here that he won his first gold medal. In the years that followed, he went on to achieve similar results. In 2007 and 2009, he competed in two Arafura Games.

In 2011, Iliesa competed in the IPC World Athletics Championships in New Zealand, where he won a silver medal; jumping a height of 1.73 metres (the equivalent to leaping over your front

door!). At this point he was ranked second in the world, which qualified him for the London 2012 Paralympic Games.

Prior to London 2012, the Pacific region had never secured that elusive gold medal at the Olympics or Paralympics. The closest they had come was in the Atlanta 1996 Games where Tongan boxer, Paea Wolfgramm, earned a silver medal and during the Beijing Paralympics in 2008 where Papua New Guinea's Francis Kompaon's had also won a silver medal for his sprint in the T46 100 metres. This was the Islands' second ever medal.

At London 2012, Lorraine Mar, Secretary General and CEO of the Fiji Association of Sports and National Olympic Committee (FASANOC) spoke of her admiration at seeing the 'noble banner blue' enter the Olympic stadium for the opening ceremony. She said, 'it couldn't have been a more prouder [sic] moment for me. The athletes and officials represented their country with pride and dignity. Going into the Games, FASANOC's aspirations for our athletes were that they compete well and deliver their best performances.'

The final of the 2012 Paralympic high-jump competition went down to the wire. Iliesa jumped 1.65 metres, which again ranked him second in the world. He then completed jumps at 1.68 metres and 1.71 metres, and crucially did so without any errors.

In the moments before his fourth and final jump, the concentration and determination in his

glassy stare are palpable. After making his way to the start point, he claps his hands and jumps once to indicate he is ready. He drops his crutches, gains momentum by hopping once on the spot, then thrusts his body forward. A series of hops propels him towards the high jump; then he dives upwards into the air, tucking his leg beneath him and somersaults over the bar. He clears 1.74 metres. The leap – a new record for Oceania and a personal best for Iliesa – is witnessed by a capacity crowd in the Olympic Arena, who roar their appreciation.

Typically, the tall Fijian accepts the applause with modesty and dignity.

But Iliesa's final jump was not enough to win the gold outright – the height had been matched by Indian competitor Girisha Hosanagara Nagarajegowda and Poland's Lukasz Mamczarz. However, because he had fewer failed jumps in the final Iliesa won the gold medal on 'count back'.

He had achieved what no other Pacific island athlete had been able to do up until that time: to win a gold medal! It could not have happened to a more modest athlete.

Lorraine Mar, who spoke on behalf of Fiji, expressed the nation's pride and admiration: 'We thank Iliesa for the glory that he has brought to his country and acknowledge him.'

Iliesa and his manager have now established the Iliesa Delana Foundation to help Fijian communities in need. The idea is to tap in to the resources and commitment of ordinary people, government, small businesses and the nation's corporations to do a lot more to tackle disadvantage in Fiji, and especially the plight of the many thousands of people who are still living below the poverty line.

Iliesa knows that changing their lives for the better will be a far bigger challenge than leaping to victory in front of 80,000 cheering people at the London Paralympics. But his ambition is to be more than just a sporting hero: he wants to use his fame to try to convince others that no disadvantage is too great to overcome, especially if Fijians work together as one.

Upper Iliesa receiving a traditional sulu alongside the Fiji President.

Lower Prime Minister Commodore Voreqe Bainimarama also thanked Delana on behalf of his government and Cabinet.

Dancing is integral to the Kiribati culture, and it has always been seen as important for young people to become good dancers. Here a dancer is photographed in traditional costume.

Opposite
Andrew Kometa and Tarieta Ruata of Kiribati. While training in Britain they were based in Crewe, Cheshire, where they experienced many new cultural activities including the excitement of having fun in the snow for the very first time.

A traditional island dance for two Kiribati boxers

KIRIBATI, a small island nestling in the central tropical Pacific Ocean, with a population of just over 100,000 is home to boxers Andrew Kometa and Tarieta Ruata. The two men aimed to represent their country at London 2012 and in doing so hoped to raise the profile of a small community struggling to survive. Climate change has had a huge impact on the island, with rising sea levels threatening to ruin the livelihoods of most of the population. Many of its inhabitants are employed in the fishing, agricultural or tourism industries, and opportunities to enter a sporting career are scarce.

It was Andrew Kometa's experiences at school which, unwittingly, began his boxing career. The other boys taunted him for being thin, so he joined the boxing club near to his home simply to build his self-esteem and physique so that he could be able to defend himself. However, his companions at the time, combined with a new-found confidence led him into a heady social life of clubbing and drinking. During these

teenage years, Andrew's life seemed to have little purpose or meaningful direction, so he made the decision to turn things around and commit his time and energy to boxing. To this day, his family still find it difficult to watch him in the ring, but through his diligence, ambition and progression, he has sustained their unwavering support. In fact, so impressed are Andrew's family with his achievements that he has triggered his younger cousin's interest in boxing, too.

Like Andrew, Tarieta Ruata has been boxing from a young age and is now in his early thirties. His father became an I-Kiribati heavyweight champion in Fiji, a significant achievement for an underfunded athlete. He was the first I-Kiribati to achieve this prestigious title. He began teaching Tarieta to box when he was 16. However, due to a lack of financial support, Tarieta was unable to compete at a higher level. However, rather than deter the youngster, this only served to make him determined to progress as far as he could.

The two boxers' paths first crossed at the Kiribati boxing gym. Tarieta was on a mission to develop the sport and to coach and encourage boys on the island to get involved. His teaching style was necessarily strict, and he encouraged self-discipline. His ethos was: 'stay and train while behaving, or go home!'

Tarieta immediately noticed Andrew's dedication and respected his assiduousness. He recalls that 'Andrew was one of the disciplined boxers, who had guts, and could take the hard

Upper
The Kiribati boxers training
hard in the hope of qualifying
for the London 2012 Olympic
Games.

Lower
A Kiribati dancer at the
farewell dance celebration
put on for the boxers by The
Kiribati Tungaru Association.

training, which went alongside his good skills, footwork and a strong body'. It didn't take Tarieta long to realise that Andrew had all the qualities he was looking for in a professional partner.

When you meet these men, you can't help but notice the remarkable bond between them; they smile a lot, which is infectious, and they clearly enjoy training together. They are also both keen to advance their spoken English and often ask, after being interviewed, whether they have improved. They also talk frequently about their desire to inspire the people back on Kiribati, and about their hopes of encouraging more young people to take up boxing. Andrew said: 'it would make me proud to do this.'

In fact, on Kiribati, there is no dedicated training facility for boxing. However, coach Derek Andrewartha allowed the boxers to train at his family home, where they made use of household items as makeshift equipment: as punch bags they used old rice bags filled with sand, and when their training shoes acquired holes they repaired them with inner tubes from old tyres. Resources were always limited: they only had three sets of gloves between them, which were beginning to wear thin in places, and which meant they often had to train without gloves, hardly conducive to high-quality training or practice.

They spent six months away from their families in the North West training camps, at Manchester Metropolitan University, Cheshire East in Crewe. Andrew explained that the camps were

very different from his training environment at home: 'It's good training here as there is a lot of equipment; they have good boxers and sparring partners, many weights, bags and rings. I think it will put us up there – back in our country we don't have a gym like this; we just train under the shade of the trees. I think it will be good to help us make it towards the Olympics.'

At home, the men have found securing funding difficult throughout their careers, including during competitions in Australia and the Delhi Commonwealth Games in 2010. Having the benefits afforded to them while staying in England brought a welcome break from these concerns.

Of course, the men had to acclimatise to the very different environment. The Kiribati Tungaru Association worked closely with Andrew and Tarieta to assist with their stay in the North West. The organisation consists of a group of people from the British Isles and Continental Europe who have family, contacts or past employment links to the Republic of Kiribati. Their aims are to facilitate good relationships between Britain and Kiribati, to welcome visitors from Kiribati to Europe, and to teach young British people about the island's culture. To fulfil these aims, the association organises social events in Britain and on the island. As a farewell celebration for the boxers, before they left Crewe to travel to Canberra to try and qualify for London 2012, the Association organised a performance of Te Reitaki, a traditional Kiribati dance.

In stark contrast to the dull miserable British weather on the day of the performance, the dancers' costumes represented the resplendent tropical island. The dancers' movements were characterised by the frigate bird, the national emblem of the country, with arms outstretched and sudden 'bird-like' movements of the head. Historically, the inhabitants did not have musical instruments, and the dance was performed to unaccompanied singing. Dancing is integral to the Kiribati culture; it has always been seen as an important accomplishment for a young person to become a good dancer. Andrew joined in with the Te Reitaki. In many ways the event encapsulated the value that the training camp had for the boxers.

Neither Andrew nor Tarieta qualified for London 2012. Andrew did achieve a silver medal in the qualifying rounds in Australia, where Tarieta also won a bronze. They both aim to inspire, and to improve the livelihoods of the youth of Kiribati. Tarieta wants to open a large gym on the island with a range of top-class facilities to encourage young boys who have gone off the rails to focus their energies on boxing. They might not have returned to their small island in the Pacific Ocean with medals, but they returned as inspiring figure-heads for other young islanders.

The traditional dancers' movements – with arms outstretched and sudden 'bird-like' movements of the head – mimic the frigate bird, the national emblem of the country. Historically, the inhabitants did not have musical instruments, and the dance was performed to unaccompanied singing.

A year 8 student from Malbank High School in Nantwich, Cheshire, proudly shows the letter he has received from his pen-pal John from Vila Central primary school in Vanuatu.

Opposite
A letter written by a Ni-Vanuatu primary school child, outlining personal hobbies and descriptions of Vanuatu for the benefit of his British pen-pal.

Schools link up across the oceans

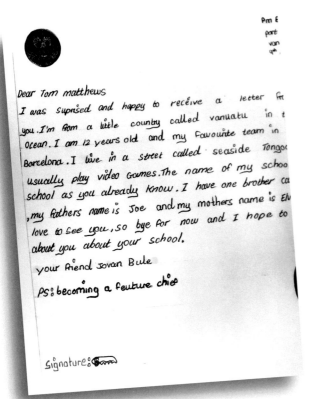

Dear Tom matthews
I was suprised and happy to receive a letter fr
you. I'm from a little country called vanuatu in t
Ocean. I am 12 years old and my favourite team in
Barcelona. I live in a street called seaside Tongoa
usually play video Games. The name of my schoo
school as you already know. I have one brother ca
, my fathers name is Joe and my mothers name is Elv
love to see you, so bye for now and I hope to
about you about your school.

your friend Jovan Bule

PS: becoming a feuture chief

Signature:

S INCE 1986, The British Friends of Vanuatu
organisation has been part of a scheme to
develop relationships between the Republic of
Vanuatu and the UK, with a view to relieving
poverty and deprivation, improving education
through scholarships, providing more accessible
primary education, and increasing the number
of books and the quantity of library materials in
Vanuatu's schools.

One high school in Cheshire has had a
particularly important role: Malbank High, which
was established over 450 years ago in the market
town of Nantwich in the borough of Cheshire
East in the UK. Malbank has 1,300 students and
proudly embraces its ethos of welcoming families
into the school community. Ahead of the Olympic
Games, the school was nominated as the '2012
School for Cheshire', which provided it with the
opportunity to extend this core ethos to other
communities overseas. One of the schools with
which it began communications was Vila Central
primary school in Vanuatu, which caters for

around 500 pupils. A sense of community is a value that both schools share: Vila Central aims to provide a friendly learning environment for young islanders and international students from Australia and New Zealand.

Malbank also had a pivotal role in the lead-up to the Olympics. The head teacher, Jeanette Walker, received the Embrace the Games Award from the Cheshire and Warrington Sports Partnership. This award was part of a scheme to acknowledge an individual's outstanding progress and contribution towards delivering a sporting legacy in connection with London 2012.

Separated by 12,000 miles they might be, but Malbank and Vila Central adopt similar techniques in actively promoting community involvement. There are, however, big differences in the resources available to their pupils. In Vanuatu, school begins early, at 7.30 a.m. and finishes at 1.30 p.m., which leaves plenty of time in the afternoon for homework, reading and leisure. The libraries at both schools are extensive and Vila Central keeps many books in their classrooms so that the students can spend time reading quietly; however, due to their popularity, the books quickly look old and tattered and there is limited funding to replace them. Malbank's head teacher Jeannette Walker was particularly interested in helping to resolve this issue and began an initiative to make it happen: 'We encouraged our pupils to give up a favourite book to send to Vanuatu. We share common priorities regarding issues with children,

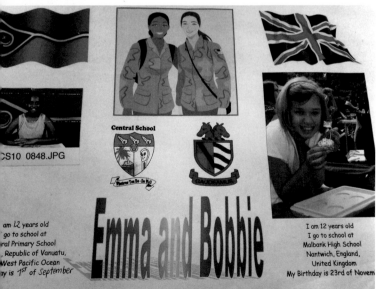

OCEANIA: AN ODYSSEY

and this was really important in our decision to develop this project.'

In addition to the book gift appeal, the students from both schools learned first-hand about each other and what life was like in their native countries. They were assigned pen-pals and exchanged letters. Malbank also made a conscious effort to incorporate information about the culture of Vanuatu into its enrichment classes. As a result, in 2011 the school's performing-arts group performed a play for the visiting Vanuatu Olympic teams, at MMUCE where they were based, which presented their ideas of what life is like on the island.

The future of this mutually beneficial relationship between the schools looks set to continue and develop in conjunction with the sporting journey of the Vanuatu athletes. The beach volleyball team hopes to compete in the Rio Olympics in 2016, which will provide both schools with an experience they can share and enjoy.

The lesson that might be drawn from the experiences of these two schools is that the legacy of Olympic involvement extends well beyond the athletes and their immediate families, and that it can lead to broad-based, long-lasting links between young people from very different backgrounds and cultures. Long may this continue.

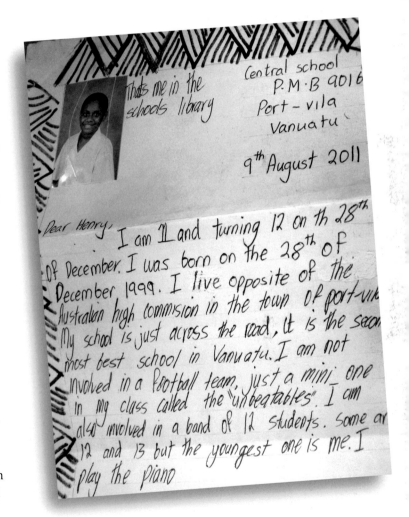

Central school
P.M.B 9016
Port - vila
Vanuatu

9th August 2011

That's me in the schools library

Dear Henry,
I am 11 and turning 12 on th 28th of December. I was born on the 28th of December 1999. I live opposite of the Australian high commision in the town of Port-vila. My school is just across the road, it is the secon most best school in Vanuatu. I am not involved in a football team, just a mini one in my class called the "unbeatables". I am also involved in a band of 12 students. Some ar 12 and 13 but the youngest one is me. I play the piano

Toea flying the flag of Papua New Guinea at the
Oceania Welcome ceremony in the heart of London:
good practice for carrying the flag later that week in
the Opening Ceremony of the Olympic Games.

*'Every time I step on to
the international platform
I feel I am contributing
to the recognition of my
country and also to the
recognition of women in
sport.'*

Pride in representing Papua New Guinea

Dika Toua lifting at the 2012 Olympics in the Excel competition centre. This was her fourth Olympic Games.

I N total eight athletes, across a range of disciplines, represented Papua New Guinea at London 2012. There were swimmers in men's butterfly and women's freestyle as well as representatives in the contact sports of judo and taekwondo, and weightlifting. Nelson Stone, meanwhile, competed in the heats of the men's 400 metres, where he clocked a season's best 46.71 seconds but failed to progress in the competition.

Some athletes were new to competition at major Games, but one weightlifter, Dika Toua, competing in the lightweight, 53 kg category, is her nation's most experienced Olympian. At 28 years old, the London 2012 Games were actually her fourth Olympic Games. As if to symbolise the blend of experience and youth, she walked alongside 24-year-old 100 metre sprinter Toea Wisil during the opening ceremony. For Toea, who had the honour of bearing their nation's flag, this was her first Olympic Games. She had run a wind-assisted personal and national best to qualify. After rugby league, weightlifting is one of Papua New Guinea's

Toea in her first-round race at London 2012, next to Allyson Felix of USA, who won Gold in the 200 and was voted the best female athlete of 2012.

most successful sports at the international level. So it was a huge honour for Dika to represent not only her country, but also this discipline so treasured by her nation, as she explained: 'There is always a sense of pride in representing my country. I am a very proud Papua New Guinean. Every time I step on to the international platform I feel I am contributing to the recognition of my country and also to the recognition of women in sport.'

Dika was ten when she began practising weightlifting at the gym next door to where she lived. When she was young she enjoyed a variety of sports: 'I had been a tomboy all my life,' she recalled, 'playing sports like netball, volleyball and rugby with my brothers in our back yard.' But weightlifting was something that she took more seriously: 'I immediately felt challenged. Being stubborn by nature, I wanted to beat the bar, so

I started to train regularly.' As soon as she was old enough, she began to compete. At the age of fifteen she took part in the 1999 South Pacific Games in Guam, were she won three silver medals. From here she began her Olympic career. A year later, she competed in the 2000 Olympic Games in Sydney. They were the first Games to feature women's weightlifting and, having gone first in the 48 kg category, she officially became the first woman ever to lift at the Games as a 16-year-old. That lift was unsuccessful, but four years later, in Athens, she finished sixth in the 53 kg division.

With her wealth of Olympic experience, Dika recalls: 'Every Olympic Games is different. Each one has its own unique stamp. I knew what to expect coming to London, but in no way did this lessen my excitement in being part of the Olympic experience. Even the competition itself is

An anxious glance at the scoreboard by Papua New Guinea's Toea Wisil is captured in this photograph of the stadium's big screen. Toea sailed through her qualifying heat.

different; you have different athletes from the last time.' She recognised that as she grew older, her approach to the Games changed: 'I came in to the London Olympics not only as an athlete but also a mother of two young children, aged 5 and 1, so my mentality and approach were different. To prepare myself I had to leave my children and my husband back home in Papua New Guinea and go to the Oceania Weightlifting Institute in New Caledonia for training. I did not see them for nearly eight months.'

Her relationship with the less-experienced Toea was almost maternal: 'Knowing exactly what it is like to compete in your first Olympics, I sympathised with all the emotions Toea was going through. I also know that by the time you get to that stage, last-minute advice is not warranted. The best thing is to be physically there to support her and for her to know that when she raced.'

Dika's advice and encouragement had a clear effect on Toea, who sailed through her qualifying heat with a time of 11.60 seconds. Six hours later she competed in the first round proper and finished fourth in her heat, 0.13 seconds behind the third-placed runner.

Toea hopes to go on and compete at the 2014 Commonwealth Games. She had previously competed in 2010 which turned out to be a stunning year for her. Not only did her photograph appear on the front of the national phonebook, but she was part of an elite group of PNG athletes invited to compete in the Asian and Indian Grand Prix Series. It was during the 3rd Grand Prix that Toea upset the favourite by taking the 100 m in 11.66 seconds. This was followed up that same season with wins in the 100 m and 200 m finals at the Oceania Championships in Cairns, Australia. However, Toea's best was yet to come when, unfancied, she placed fourth in the Commonwealth Games 100 m final in Delhi. She also has 100, 200 and 400 metre gold medal titles to defend at the next Pacific Games, which will take place on home soil at Port Moresby, Papua New Guinea, in 2015.

Dika is now planning a life after her weightlifting career finishes, while also preparing for the 2014 Commonwealth Games: 'Whilst I am training in New Caledonia I am also doing a coaching diploma. By Rio 2016 I will be 32 years of age. I would like to try for my fifth Olympics, but that depends on my fitness levels. If I am not there as an athlete then maybe I will be there as a coach.' However she represents Papua New Guinea in 2016, she will be remembered as Papua New Guinea's 'queen of weightlifting'.

These two Papua New Guinea women athletes, at different stages of their careers, share a gritty determination to compete at the highest level. Along with all their compatriots, they have carried the hopes of a nation with pride and honour.

'*... when Islanders come together we stick together, we act as one.*'

Fijian Judoka Josateki Naulu, on the mat at London 2012 against Srdjan Mrvaljevic of Montenegro.

Coaching one big judo family

Guam's Ric Blas Jnr photographed alongside Vanuatu judo coach Brett Wright.

T H E home of judo is the 'dojo', which in Japanese means 'the place of the way'. The sport is now 130 years old. The eight Judokas representing Oceania stayed in the Kendal dojo, in the South Lakeland area of north-west England, where they were guided by the expertise of their coach, Mike Liptrot. The athletes came from Vanuatu, Palau, the Solomon Islands, Guam, Samoa, Papua New Guinea, Fiji and American Samoa. Upon their arrival in Kendal, they quickly became like a family: one of the most experienced judokas, Jennifer Anson, from Palau (the only female in the group) recalled: 'Once I met the guys I felt like I was at home, when Islanders come together we stick together, we act as one.' The staff at the dojo created individual programmes for each of the athletes to cater for both their sport's needs and to help them acclimatise.

Team coach Mike Liptrot first began attending the Kendal Judo Club when he was six and has enjoyed a lengthy career in the sport. It was his own coach, Tony Macconnell, who encouraged him

to become a coach: 'I was 13 years old when Tony came to live in my town. He was then the British team manager and was to be the main influence in my competitive career. I was a member of the British team for 10 years, was a medalist at the German Open and had medals from all over Great Britain and Europe, in the 1980s. I trained full time in the town, travelling to Japan and throughout Europe. This without doubt was the highlight of my sporting career. The day I finished full-time training Tony said to me, "don't worry lad you're gonna have a great time. You have been a great player but you will be a better coach than you were ever a player."'

Mike was an ideal person to head up the Oceania judo team, having previously coached at the Youth Olympic Games and, during his competitive career, his working relationships had extended to Oceania, where he had met Ricardo Blas Senior, who is now secretary general of the Oceania National Olympic Committees, the father of one of the judokas, Ricardo Blas Junior. Ricardo Blas Senior competed as a judoka for Guam at the 1988 Summer Olympics in Seoul, coming joint-19th in the men's heavyweight competition. Having known Mike previously, he could say with confidence that, 'to have Mike involved in the preparation for these athletes is great, as we can see the differences he is making'.

Mike acted as a parental guardian to the athletes; as well as his main job as coach, he made breakfast, chauffeured them to events in

OCEANIA: AN ODYSSEY

a minibus, and introduced them to the English social scene. He also bought each member a mobile phone to ensure they could have regular contact with their families. He aimed to acculturate them, as well as help them prepare for the Games: 'for many of these athletes, they are the first in their country to compete in Judo at an Olympic Games. This is not just massive for them, but it's a big step for their countries and opens doors for generations afterwards.'

The athletes looked to Mike as a role model and respected his knowledge. Nazario Fiakaifonu, judoka from Vanuatu, has described Mike as 'the best judoka coach I have ever seen; he was there for us, he made us better athletes, he taught us "the passion of sport" and the reason why we are all doing this. As well as learning about technique, I learned more about myself and the best way for me to train to get the best out of me. Mike taught us about creativity, artistry and learning the real mastery of Judo.'

Ricardo Blas Junior shares this belief in the coach: 'Mike has the experience and has the best preparation for major events, and you can see his training and advice worked.'

In an acknowledgement of his competence and value as a coach, Mike was asked to become ONOC's official coaching advisor for the 2012 Games with a remit to provide support to other judo coaches. He recalls that: 'some of the athletes didn't come with the correct judo suits, so we made sure they all had the correct equipment; and

some of the coaches forgot to bring suits, which they need to sit in the matches, so I went out and made sure they were ready to support their athlete.'

During their events members of the team delivered notable performances: Tony Lomo, from the Solomon Islands, in the −60 kg category, came top in his first-round match, beating his competitor from Mozambique to advance to the round of 16. He then competed against a judoka who was then ranked sixth in the world in Sofiane Milous of France. Sadly, Lomo lost this bout, missing out on a quarter-final place. Ricardo Blas Junior also reached the round of 16 before being knocked out. Afterwards, he was able to maintain perspective: 'I got into the second round. I am pleased with how I have performed at the Games.'

After the Games, Mike expressed his pride in the Oceania competitors' achievements: 'the guys really have done well, these Games were all about development; they did really well.' Nazario Fiakaifonu expressed his enjoyment of the whole experience: 'These Olympics have created pictures and memories for me I will never forget, it has made me realise my dream.'

Mike continues to be in regular contact with all of the team to monitor their progress and offer support, with a view to the athletes competing at future Games, helping to demonstrate yet again how important all of the coaching and support staff are in helping the athletes perform to the best of their ability on the biggest stage.

OCEANIA: AN ODYSSEY

Oceania judo coach and father figure Mike Liptrot pictured with Nazario from Vanuatu and Palau judo coach Ngiratmetuchl Belechel in the Athletes' Village during London 2012. After working with the Oceania judokas in the Pre-Games Training Camps Mike was asked to be ONOC's official coaching advisor for the 2012 Games.

Oceania swimmers pose for a photograph together while training in Liverpool before London 2012. From left to right, Giordan, Keesha, Kerson Hadley, Ching Mau Wei, Debra Daniel, Paul Elaisa, Matelita Buadromo, Ann-Marie Hepler.

Riding the Olympic waves: Giordan Harris and the Marshallese

'I followed my best friend and joined the swim team. I was terrible at first, but I had a love for the water which has carried me to where I am today.'

T H E Republic of the Marshall Islands is located in the northern Pacific Ocean, in the Micronesia area of Oceania. It consists of no fewer than 1,156 islands and islets and has a population of 68,000. Administratively it is linked closely to the USA, who maintain a small military presence on the islands and from which the republic continues to receive a significant amount of financial aid. Despite this, average incomes remain low, and the infrastructure relatively undeveloped. Athletes from the Marshall Islands, it would be fair to say, have a lot to contend with.

Despite this, three of the four Marshallese who represented their country at London 2012 came away with season, or personal, best performances: Haley Nemra in the women's 800 m; Ann-Marie Hepler in the 50 m freestyle; and, in the corresponding men's event, Giordan Harris.

In many ways Giordan Harris typifies the Oceania Olympic adventure, battling and yet overcoming lack of facilities, finance and support. He comes from the tiny island of Ebeye, which

Giordan at one year of age. This is when his family realised he was a 'water baby', someone born in the islands who is always drawn to the ocean. As a baby he would always crawl to the reef to get to the water, and his family had to pay close attention to his whereabouts.

Giordan, aged eight, featured on the front page of the local Kwajalein team magazine *Swim*.

SWIM MAGAZINE

The Kwajalein Sports News

Who Will Be Kwaj's Fastest?

RECORDS FALL AT MILLICAN POOL !!!

6 Steps To Building A Better Backstroke

MAKOS VS BARRACUDAS !

Official Magazine of the Kwajalein Swim Team

April 2002

Giordan Harris
Makos

SECRETS OF THE FLIP TURN

Best Swimmers In The South Pacific...

PICKS, PREVIEWS AND PROJECTIONS:

PRICE: $5.99 ($8.99 RMI)
DISPLAY UNTIL MAY 15, 2002

ACTION PAK PHOTO MAGAZINES

NEXT STOP: Micronesian Games...

is just a mile long but has a population of over 15,000. There is no running water on Ebeye, and the population experiences frequent power shortages. Nevertheless, Giordan loves island life: 'I have been to countries all over the world, and nothing is like island life. Waking up to the sun every morning; having 90-degree weather all year round. Some people hate it; I personally love it.'

He first learned to swim in the sea when he was six. One advantage of living on such a small island was that he was never very far from the sea or a place to practise. Giordan explained that, when he was young, it was swimming with his childhood best friend David Valen that sparked his love for the sport: 'David had joined the swim team on Kwajalein, the island on which we both had attended school. Naturally, I followed my best friend and joined the swim team. I was terrible at

When he was six years old Giordan started swimming in the Kwajalein team. The first-place ribbons in the scrap book are from the age of eight upwards.

Below right
This photograph shows the American base pool where the Kwajalein team would train. In the lead-up to London 2012, Giordan travelled three miles by boat twice a day to this, the only pool on the Marshall Islands. It looks idyllic, but the salt water in this pool did not provide ideal training for the fresh water in the Olympic pool.

first, but I had a love for the water ... that love for the water has carried me to where I am today in my swim career.'

Ebeye does not have a swimming pool of its own, so during Giordan's preparation for the Olympics he travelled twice a day to the only pool on the Marshall Islands, in Kwajelein. Kwajalein is three miles away by boat, and the pool is located in an American military base. This often made it difficult for Giordan to train: 'Many people have asked me about how difficult it is to get to practice, and, yeah, I've missed practices, but I always make up for it. In the event that I couldn't make it to Kwajalein, I would go to the ocean and train there. All because I fell in

The results board at London 2012. Despite being warned that he might not make the starting blocks at London 2012 due to an injury, Giordan was determined he would recover and race in London. He achieved a time of 26.88 seconds, a new personal best.

The moment Giordan had been waiting for: the start gun fires, and he dives into the pool for his 50 m heat.

OCEANIA: AN ODYSSEY

These two photographs capture some of Giordan's most memorable moments: demonstrating his pride competing for the Marshall Islands in the Aquatics Centre; and standing next to the symbolic Olympic flame in the Olympic Stadium.

It is believed that the javelin throw has featured in the Olympics since 708 BC, so Leslie is following in a long and proud tradition.

Leslie Copeland, Fijian javelin thrower

'I have always dreamt of competing with the best. I set out a goal to reach the Olympic Games and fulfil my dreams.'

V ATUKOULA, a small town on the north coast of Fiji, is home to javelin thrower Leslie Copeland. This is where he spent his childhood years growing up with his siblings. After his father passed away when Leslie was just nine, his aunt became a great support to the family.

Leslie believes it was this support that encouraged his progress throughout his career: 'My family support me in everything, so growing up in Fiji and around my family members really helped me a lot in my throwing. They understood how much I wanted to reach the highest level of my sport and they made it their goal to see me achieve it. I was brought up in a family where we did not have much, but were always thankful for whatever we achieved and received. My family taught me that with everything we do, we should always be thankful to the Lord for his kindness.'

Leslie's cultural background and religion also influenced his attitude towards training and encouraged him to pursue his sporting objective: 'My culture offered me peace and direction

towards my goals. My religion and faith allowed me to believe that everything is possible through God.' Leslie prays often: 'before every lift of a weight and every throw. When I find things difficult, I turn to the Lord for guidance and support. My faith allows me to achieve things that are beyond my dreams.'

He initially discovered his talent for javelin throwing during his first year of high school at Marist Brothers High School. Here he realised he was able to throw farther than his peers: 'I have always dreamt of competing with the best in the world. With that in mind, I set out a goal to reach the Olympic Games and fulfil my dreams of competing amongst the best.'

Leslie's education has always been important to him, but striking a balance between his school work and his training was difficult. For three years he was taught mathematics and English by his teacher Ms Vakaliwaliwa, whom he believes had a huge influence on his education. Similarly, her reflections about Leslie as a young student reveal an early determination: 'He was very humble. He lived humbly. He shared with me some of the hardships: both financial and social. He shared with me and I found out more. He had the love for the sport. Very few of us knew that he was giving his all on the ground, at the same time when he stayed late, he did not have enough bus fare to take him home. I'm not surprised to see Leslie at the top, because he had it in him then. He made do with what he had.'

Olympian Leslie Copeland
on the Fijian coastline
sitting on a traditional Fijian
outrigger canoe.

At home training among the palm trees: the bumpy terrain did not provide ideal conditions for his run-up.

Between the ages of 14 and 19, from 2002 to 2005, Leslie took part in the Coca Cola Games, where, each year, he surpassed the national record for the javelin throw. He also competed in the shot-putt event. The Games are the world's biggest school athletic sporting meet and provide young Fijian sports enthusiasts with the opportunity to display their athletic skills. Leslie recalls: 'I competed in all the Coca Cola Games from when I was in form three right up to form six, and that's where my love for javelin started. I just threw and threw and I surpassed all the records in high school and then that made me want to go further and beat the Fiji record.'

Between his major competitions in 2002 and 2005 he increased the distance of this throws enormously, from 46 metres to 67 metres. It was then that Leslie was spotted by Lorraine Mar, Secretary General and CEO of the Fiji Association of Sports and National Olympic Committee (FASANOC) and Yvonne Mullins, the Executive Director of the Oceania Athletics Association.

Yvonne believes that Leslie has one of the biggest personalities of any athlete she has worked with: 'He has grown from an enthusiastic young boy to a fine young man who still has so much potential. Leslie has been on a number of sports teams that I have been involved with and has always had a positive influence on fellow team members. He is a high achiever with much to offer the sport and we look forward to watching him over the years as he reaches his full potential. She

believes his relationship with his coach, James Goulding, is one of the success stories of Athletics Fiji and hopes that, in the future, Leslie will also turn his hand to coaching.

James Goulding was an experienced javelin thrower himself. However, his coaching experience came from Fijian schools where he used to help the children with their technique during sports days. Having only previously coached school children, James found coaching Leslie to be a challenge: 'When Leslie and I set out on his journey to try and qualify for the Olympics, it was a huge ask. I had only coached at a very junior level. When I took up all the responsibility to try

to improve the standards, there was a lot I had to learn. And one of the things I had to learn was to listen to him.'

The most popular sport in Fiji is rugby and, as such, it receives the greatest amount of funding. In comparison, javelin is seen as a relatively minor discipline and it receives little financial support. In Fiji, therefore, Leslie found it difficult to find other talented athletes with whom to practise. He had little choice but to travel to Australia, which was a struggle for him to fund, but it was worth it because the support structures there were excellent. He believes that his experiences with Australian athletes were invaluable to him: 'These

Leslie and his coach James Goulding in the Athletes' Village during London 2012.

Leslie, photographed with Tuvaluan sprinters, T'noa and Asenate, as they take on local schoolchildren and volunteers at the University of Central Lancashire in Preston.

competitions enhanced my abilities and opened my eyes to the world of javelin throwing.' Due to the cost of travel, his competitions abroad were limited to only three or four a year.

In 2009, Leslie secured official sponsorship from a well-known energy-drink manufacturer, and with their financial backing he was able to compete more often: 'I sat with my coach James Goulding and we drew up a plan to reach the Olympic Games in London. With only our faith and determination, we started on our journey. My coach and I started to see a lot of improvements in my training and throws, and I became more confident in myself and achieving my goals.'

In 2010, after noticeable improvements to his throwing ability, FASANOC offered him an International Olympic Committee (IOC)

scholarship. The IOC decided to award athletes these scholarships, two years prior to the Olympics, if they demonstrate the potential to qualify for an Olympic event. Altogether, four Fijian athletes were awarded Olympic Scholarships for Athletes 2012. Through the scholarship, Leslie received funding to assist with his training and preparations, as well as with his living expenses at home. He also utilised the funding to travel overseas to train and take part in international competitions.

Alongside his sporting career, Leslie also has a full-time job as a civil-engineering technician. He completed a diploma at the Fiji Institute of Technology and hopes to achieve a degree in the subject: 'What I love about civil engineering is the challenges it offers. Being able to solve someone else's problems gives me much pleasure in the field.'

At home, Leslie trained at Fiji's National Stadium in Suva, 190 km away on the opposite side of the island, where the track was severely damaged due to constant wear. Bumps and cracks were visible across it and, to avoid them, he was unable to move in a straight line while executing his run-up. He explained that, 'There is a big risk in training. If I land here [on a break in the track], I can twist my ankle but I'm happy with what I have, I can't complain.'

Despite these difficulties, Leslie prefers to practise at home: 'I feel comfortable training here. I can train overseas, with better facilities, but I seem to love training here mostly. I've tried training overseas and it did not work for me so I think being around my family and friends works for me. This is where I come and be myself. It's always a relief to get back home.'

Refurbishment work began on the Suva stadium just prior to London 2012, which meant that it was closed in March. For that reason Leslie travelled to Europe to train: 'I was frustrated as I could not use the facility to fully prepare myself before leaving Fiji.' The stadium will gain a new grandstand to cover seating, as well as showers, bathrooms, and new playing surfaces; the track will also be repaired. In the future it will be acceptable for international competition in athletics and rugby. Leslie hopes that 'the new look of the National Stadium can attract more competitions and competitors from abroad so they can enjoy the hospitality of the Fijian people'.

An experience that Leslie remembers fondly, and one he believes was of great benefit to his career, was the time he spent at the Pre-Games Training Camps in England, at the University of Central Lancashire. Through this arrangement, Leslie says he 'was able to make use of all the facilities, hospitality and assistance that UCLan had to offer. The support team were so impressive and I will never forget them for their hospitality. I love the North West; the green environment reminds me of home.'

Like the other Oceania athletes, Leslie stayed in student halls of residence at the university, close

enough to The Sir Thomas Finney Sport Centre where Leslie enjoyed training. Sports development coaching experts and sports-science students at UCLan provided a support network for him. They also helped him to recover from a shoulder injury he sustained during practice. His one regret was that he 'only wished to have competed more in the UK in the lead up to the Olympics'.

Lorraine Mar believes that UCLan assisted Leslie to qualify for the World Championships: 'It is expensive for the athletes to travel to Australia and New Zealand, even though they are only a few hours away. The arrangement formed with the North West UK is fantastic. The benefit for Leslie was huge. He came to the North West last year [in 2010] for two or three weeks and almost immediately after that he went on to competitions

Leslie having fun dressing in traditional English costume at the historic Old Hall in Tatton Park during a farewell event for all Pacific island athletes training in the North West before they were to travel down to London for the Olympic Games.

and I'm pleased to say that he actually qualified for the World Championships in Korea.' Crucially, here he threw 76.57 metres, which then qualified him automatically for the Olympics.

A few weeks before the competition started at London 2012 Leslie commented: 'I was delighted and more determined to keep on moving forward towards the Olympics. I want to walk out of the Olympic Stadium knowing that I have done, with no regrets, done everything that I could have. Everything I've been taught; execute everything I can do to the best of my ability; just doing the best that's possible; attempting the impossible.'

Taking part in the Opening Ceremony, on 27 July 2012, was, he explained, the pinnacle of his journey: 'At that moment I knew that I had achieved my sporting goal. The atmosphere during the opening ceremony was incredible; it was

everything I had hoped for and more. Walking out into a crowd of more than 75,000 people screaming is something that I will never forget.'

Before his event, on 8 August, Leslie returned to Preston (UCLan) to train, rather than remain in the Athletes' Village as he needed to practise in a calm environment. His strategy was to 'treat it as a normal competition', he explained. 'I don't want to get too excited; I might just lose my head.'

Coming in to the Olympics, Leslie was ranked 43 out of 44. However, this all changed after his event where he threw a massive 80.19 m in qualification. He only just missed out by one place (and by just 10 cm) on qualifying for the final round of the twelve top-ranking athletes. Ironically, if he had managed to qualify for the next round to compete in the final, and thrown the same distance, he would have been ranked 10th at the Olympics.

After the event, Leslie expressed his disappointment: 'I was so unlucky to have fallen 20 centimetres short of qualifying for the finals and becoming the first ever Fijian athlete to qualify for the last round of the Olympic Games in athletics.'

However, he acknowledged that this was still a great achievement. He went on to say that his overall Olympic experience 'was worth the wait and all the struggles along the way. From a small island in the Pacific to the heart of the United Kingdom, I feel blessed to have been a part of the London 2012 Olympic Games.'

Leslie is focused as he trains hard to achieve his sporting ambitions.

The day the Nauru boxers met Sir Charles
Allen, London 2012 Board Member. Ian Irwin,
D.J. Maaki, Sir Charles Allen, coach Tim Aki,
Joseph Deiragera, Colin Caleb, Jake Ageidu.

Nauru Boxing Federation
Logo designed for the
Kendal Camp and placed on
anoraks for the Nauru Team.

Eager to learn: four boxers of Nauru

'When the boxers arrived in Kendal, Ian could tell that they found it difficult to adjust.'

I N August 2011, Kendal, a beautiful countryside market town located in the South Lakeland District of Cumbria, in the north-west of England, became, over a number of months, the temporary home to the Nauruan boxing team ahead of the London 2012 Olympics. The team consisted of four young men: Jake Ageidu, Joseph Deiragera, Colin Caleb, and D.J. Maaki.

Back on Nauru, all four men work in the only supermarket on the island. Sean Oppenheimer, the president of the Nauru Boxing Federation and the most successful businessman in Nauru, also happens to own the supermarket. Nauru has a high unemployment rate, so the boys are in a privileged position in having secure jobs as well as Oppenheimer's support. He believes that sport is beneficial to the Nauruan people and wanted to ensure that the boxers had a steady income in order to buy decent food, training equipment, and the means to travel abroad to train ahead of 2012.

In 2010 Ian Irwin was asked by the Nauruan Boxing Federation to coach the boys. Ian was

by then semi-retired from a successful career coaching the Great Britain boxing team. During his career, he had taken the GB team to three Olympics: Barcelona, in 1992; Atlanta, in 1996; and Sydney in 2000, where Audley Harrison had won a gold medal. The Federation specifically wanted someone with a vast amount of experience, which fitted Ian's style of coaching perfectly. Having retired at the peak of his career and with no other major commitments for the foreseeable future, Ian embraced the opportunity to coach the Nauruan team.

In the late 1950s, when Ian was growing up in Ambleside, a small town 13 miles from Kendal, he was a regular visitor to the YMCA where boxing was hugely popular. In Nauru it is more difficult to follow the sport due to a lack of equipment and a limited social media network: Nauru, for example, only has one fortnightly newspaper. However, Oppenheimer does what he can to raise money for the boxers. He regularly holds a public raffle on the island. The boxers' families have also supported them with travel costs, and thanks to the media coverage the team has received in the UK, public support and funding have increased. However, Ian believes that Nauru still has a long way to go to provide the team with what is needed to improve their performance: 'Nauru is [still] very much in need of better training facilities, frequent quality sparring and increased competition,' he explains.

Ian relates how difficult it was for the boxers to dedicate time to practise when they were working

Boxers in Nauru bouncing on tyres in the gym as part of the training programme to improve balance and core stability.

full-time. They would take early morning runs or meet in the evening at the gym after work. The gym is a large corrugated-iron construction made up largely of asbestos, and there are no showers. The boxers have to collect water from tubs outside if they wish to wash themselves down. This is a stark contrast to the Kendal Judo Club, where the team trained in England. Ian points out that, 'there are four boxing clubs on the island, all very small, in sheds. There's a boxing ring and only a few punch bags, nothing else. It's a bit of a health hazard really [referring to the asbestos]. If it was in the UK it would have been closed down due to health and safety.'

He has identified a run-down government building on Nauru which he believes has the potential to be redeveloped as a gym (he should know; his first job was in the building trade). The government wants to transform it into an Olympic centre of excellence for weight-governed sports (weightlifting, boxing, judo and wrestling), and Ian hopes to be working with the boys there to prepare for the Glasgow Commonwealth Games in 2014 and the Rio Olympics in 2016.

When the boxers arrived in Kendal, they were shy, and Ian could tell that they found it difficult to adjust to their new surroundings. This was something Ian, himself, could relate to; in 1960, when he himself competed in the Junior Amateur Boxing Association in London, where he reached the semi-final, it had been his first trip to the capital. Remembering his experience and

Middle
The boxers receive feedback at the end of the training session in Nauru.

Bottom
Nauru Boxing Federation centre.

Bottom
A joint judo and boxing
training session at Kendal
Judo Club.

feelings about London at the time helped him to identify with the boxers' uncertainty about their new environment: 'There weren't even any traffic lights in Ambleside and Windermere [at that time], so walking up out of the Underground [in London] and seeing all those lights flashing was just mesmerizing, and frightening.' With this in mind he says, 'I took a softly, softly approach so I could have a look at their abilities. It wasn't a case of pushing them until the point of killing them. There had to be an element of enjoyment in it.'

The North West's training camps served several purposes for the athletes: the development of the boxers' sporting performance and their experience through competition, and it facilitated their acclimatisation to what was referred to in a post-training camp report as the 'changing weather conditions' in the United Kingdom. They trained three sessions per day and, while this occupied most of their time, during their stay the team visited Manchester United Football Club and toured the ground. They also experienced their

OCEANIA: AN ODYSSEY

first snowfall. The boxers had seen photographs of snow before, but they had never experienced the fun of snowballing and making snowmen.

The use of technology at the camps was invaluable to the boxers while they practised. 'Clickers', an electronic scoring system, was introduced, which the boxers found to be a brilliant motivational tool. Local boxing clubs, in conjunction with Kendal Judo Club, organised a boxing tournament to provide the boxers with more experience of competition. This event also raised funding for the boxers: two hundred paying spectators attended the tournament, the proceeds of which paid for boxing gloves and head guards. Each boxer's contest was filmed by the Judo Club and played back for analysis at the next training session.

Ian used innovative techniques during training: the judo club acquired a large, 8 × 4 foot wall-mounted mirror from a local glazing firm, which the team used for shadow boxing. He also introduced a training diary to document food and fluid intake and to check the boxers' weight in the morning, when they were at their lightest, and then after each subsequent training session. Ian explained: 'If you have a record of when you've felt absolutely brilliant and buzzing, then you can go through that routine next time. [However], it didn't go down too easily at first.' Due to the variety of food Kendal has to offer, maintaining the boxers' weight was an issue. The Nauruan people eat rice-based meals three times a day due to its

affordability. Ian quickly realised that structuring the boxers' diet was a challenge to their cultural values as they had learnt to eat in moderation on the island, as he explained: 'if there is more than one child in the family why should the boxer get a better diet than the rest, it stops me from saying to them "you should not eat that but eat this' knowing the family probably cannot afford it. This no doubt can affect energy systems and, of course, making the competition weight.'

However, the team quickly got used to and took advantage of the variety of food available in Kendal. The post-training camp report commented

Top left English Institute of Sport in Sheffield, the home of GB Olympic boxing. Ian took the boxers to meet the GB squad.

Top right Young boxers in Nauru with Ian Irwin, Sean Oppenheimer (President of Nauru Boxing) and the Cuban Foreign Minister.

Bottom left In Kendal, Jake shadow boxing in front of a large mirror.

Bottom right Ian working with Colin on pad work training in the ring in Kendal.

Colin Caleb in Kendal boxing
tournament February 2012.

D.J. Maaki boxing in Kendal, July 2011.

that, 'there was nothing the boxers wouldn't eat'. Consequently, circuit training and running on the hills in the area around Kendal Castle became a large part of their exercise routines. Initially, the boxers' attitude to training was more carefree than Ian's: 'In the very early days, punctuality was a big problem. They were a little laid-back on the island, as if tomorrow never comes. I told them, as nicely as I could, that, if I can get here on time then you can too.'

Ian also hoped that while they were in Britain, the athletes would utilise the time to improve their English: 'There were times when I was with them and they would be talking together in Nauruan. I wanted them to learn English and use it. In twenty years' time they might find speaking English the difference between getting a job or not and I didn't want them to regret not learning it.'

In order to train in the North West and elsewhere, Jake, the eldest boxer, left his wife and newborn son in Nauru. This was clearly difficult for him. Ian recalls that, during training, 'he kept it all to himself, but he certainly missed the family'.

The team took part in their most successful Pacific Games to date, in New Caledonia in 2011, in which they came third having accumulated three bronze medals, three silver and a gold, which was achieved by Jake in the 91 kg+ event. He was invited to take part in another training camp in Azerbaijan, but Ian explains that, 'He didn't go,

Upper Ian Irwin in Nauru with President Marcus Stephen and Boxing Federation President Sean Oppenheimer.

Lower Nauru boxers shadow boxing their way through a technical session.

which is a real shame; he missed out there, but the family has to come first. We all learned a lesson from that.'

In July 2011 the team spent time in Sheffield, in South Yorkshire, with the GB boxing squad, whom Ian used to coach. Ian has stated that this was a pivotal point in his relationship with the team, who had previously been somewhat resistant to his teaching methods: 'The fact I used to head up that [GB] squad, improved their confidence in me. Slowly they gained an understanding of what was required to reach the top. It gave them a more positive frame of mind, from an "I will try and do it" to an "I will do it" attitude.' This experience also improved their technique: 'Just being invited to the GB Squad and sparring three rounds with some of the best boxers in the world did their confidence a great deal of good. But also, they understood when I talked about "raising the bar".'

Unfortunately, none of the four boxers qualified for the Games. D.J. and Jake did not compete in the qualifiers as Ian felt they were not physically ready. Both Joe and Colin reached the semi-finals of their respective qualifying tournaments, but Colin lost to Australian boxer Luke Jackson, who then qualified for London 2012. 'They've a long way to go,' concluded Ian, 'but, whether their journey would lead to disappointment or glory was always irrelevant. They came away with a great experience that they will never forget, and that, right there, overshadows the results.'

Ann-Marie during the Opening Ceremony, having proudly represented the Marshall Islands in the athletes' parade around the stadium. Confetti floated down during the GB team's entrance, while David Bowie's 'Heroes' was played loudly.

'We're just two friends, swimming, trying to swim as fast as we can. She's faster than me, and I don't really mind.'

Ann-Marie in the Aquatics Centre in the London Olympic Park, waving a banner for her team mate Giordan Harris.

Four Oceania swimmers together all the way

Five Oceania swimmers: Judith Meauri from Papua New Guinea; Keesha Keane from Palau, Ann-Marie Hepler from the Marshall Islands; Debra Daniel from the Federated States of Micronesia (who swam in a different heat), and Celeste Brown from the Cook Islands.

THE London Olympics contained over 30 swimming events; so the chances of four Oceania athletes competing in the same heat would appear to be extremely remote? Remarkably, however, that is just what happened in the women's 50 metre freestyle on 3 August. The four athletes representing their countries were Judith Meauri from Papua New Guinea; Ann-Marie Hepler from Marshall Islands; Keesha Keane from Palau; and Celeste Brown from the Cook Islands.

This was the first time any of the four girls had competed in the Olympics, and having the benefit of each other's support made their experience even more special. All of the girls had met before, during competitions prior to the Olympics, and the fact that they were familiar with each other's backgrounds, including the funding difficulties each had faced along the way, quickly cemented their friendship. The girls had a clear understanding of how hard each would have worked to reach this stage in their careers: 'Competing against each other I think pushes us

The entire Marshall Islands Olympic Delegation photographed on the London Eye after competition was over. Athletes include sprinters Timi Garstang, Haley Nemra and swimmers Giordan Harris and Ann-Marie Hepler.

The Oceania swimmers undertaking stretching exercises during a training session in Liverpool.

all to work harder', Ann-Marie Helper commented, 'We give each other support.'

Ann-Marie and Keesha Keane first met in Palau, but it was not until they competed together in Shanghai during the 2011 World Championships that they became close friends. Subsequently, they both trained at the North West camps in England at a regional pool in Liverpool: 'Keesha and I race together a lot in different competitions,' Ann-Marie explained, 'it's either her or me that comes out on top.' But the girls agree that they are not competitive:

'We don't really think about competing against each other', Keesha said.

'We're just two friends, swimming, trying to swim as fast as we can. She's faster than me, and I don't really mind.'

To which Ann-Marie replied: 'She'll beat me one day!'

Having each other there at the Olympics made their experiences all the more fulfilling and enjoyable. It made training easier 'because we all know each other', Keesha reflected. 'If we have something we're doing wrong or we don't understand it, our friends could tell us and we'd listen to them because we're friends.' And in between training they were able to "goof off, [and] have fun",' Ann-Marie confessed.

OCEANIA: AN ODYSSEY

The four Marshall Islands Olympic athletes: Timi Garstan (runner), Haley Nemra (runner), Ann-Marie Hepler (swimmer) and Giordan Harris (swimmer) at the Opening Ceremony, dressed in traditional Marshallese clothing including a 'wut' (head dress) and a 'marmar' (necklace).

All four swimmers were extremely nervous before the big race, but being together helped Ann-Marie to relax: 'We talked to each other in the call room; it got my mind off of the race [but] I don't know about her [looking to Keesha],' she laughed.

'I kept thinking about the race,' Keesha admitted, laughing.

'We walked out and my eyes were on the crowd,' Ann-Marie explained, 'I didn't let them get to me. I just took off my tracksuit and shoes and slapped my legs and arms to wake my muscles up, then I stood on the blocks and focused on my race. I blanked everybody out, and when the buzzer went, I just went for it.'

Judith finished first out of the four and came second overall. Ann-Marie followed closely behind her (in third) while Keesha came next (fourth) and then Celeste, who finished seventh.

The girls were very pleased with their results in the race, with Ann-Marie beating her personal best, as she reflected afterwards: 'My entry time was 28.43 seconds, and I got 28.06, so I got my personal best and I'd never got near that time before, all my hard work over the last months and years paid off.'

Sharing their Olympic experiences was fantastic in every sense. Keesha recalled that, 'There were so many times when we did stupid things and also fun things that make it memorable.' These young women were given an opportunity not extended to many people: to compete together on a world stage.

The girls are now looking forward to doing it all over again at the next Olympics in Rio de Janeiro in 2016; and they hope that their experiences will inspire the next generation of swimmers from Oceania.

Every Olympic nation was welcomed to the Athletes' Village by vibrantly dressed jester-like dancers who entered the ceremony singing their own rendition of 'Bicycles' by Queen. Dancers, dressed to the theme of Shakespearean Britain, circled on bicycles, ringing hand-bells in time to the song, as they gathered the athletes before the podium from which the Mayor of the Athletes' Village greeted them.

The view from the London Organising Committee

I T may be the smallest continent in the Olympic Movement, but Joanna (Jojo) Ferris tells us how Oceania punched above its weight on the road to London 2012.

'Having worked with the Oceania National Olympic Committees in Fiji for four years as the Founding Manager of the Sports Training and Outreach Program on HIV (STOP HIV), it was an exciting prospect being offered the role of Oceania Regional Manager for LOCOG. Although I knew it was an extraordinary opportunity, it wasn't an easy decision. First, I wanted to make sure that STOP HIV would be in safe hands which, I am pleased to say, was very quickly achieved with ONOC hiring Margaret Eastgate as the manager of the program. Second, I knew this was a chance to represent Oceania in a global context and to ensure that Oceania's preparation for an Olympic Games was the best yet, which was both an exciting yet extremely daunting prospect.

'Two weeks into the job, in August 2010, having come from Fiji, London's summer already felt

Fiji's Judoka Sisilia with young people at the London 2012 World Sport Day. Sisi trained in Kendal at a Pre-Games Training Camp for six months.

cold; there was no space to breathe on the Tube; people looked at me strangely when I said hello; and the taxis didn't stop when I tried to hail them (until I worked out a ssss and low hand movement needed to be adjusted). I received an email one morning from the CEO from Vanuatu's National Olympic Committee reminding me that "I can always come home to the sunshine!" It made me miss the Pacific, but resolute that I would stay and do the best I could for Oceania's preparation. I was committed to representing the region within LOCOG and demonstrating what Oceania was capable of.

'Knowing that Oceania often falls off the Magellan maps, I arrived in London and pinned our version of the Pacific up at my desk. This one places Oceania at the centre of the world and reminded everyone where our focus was. I also ensured the LOCOG Beach Volleyball sport managers had the anthem of Vanuatu (just in case) and sent them a fact every day about Vanuatu to encourage them to follow the Beach Volleyball girls more closely leading up to the Invitational Test Event. As we were a small team we extended our meetings to include the Oceania coordinators from Sport Entries, Accreditation and Press Accreditation. Everything I learned from working in the Pacific region about being generous and welcoming I tried to apply to create our LOCOG 'Oceania Family', and it was extremely rewarding come Games time to hear them educating their colleagues about the region

and working so well with each of the National Olympic Committees.

'With a 12-hour time difference, I was often working late into the night or waking up early morning to make phone calls and I remember one night in the office, pitch dark outside with snow falling, I waited to make a call to Kiribati and Fiji National Olympic Committees. There were only two other people in the office, and one was convinced I had stayed back late so I could call my friends or family using the work phones. It took some time to convince them that I was making a work call because it sounded like I was enjoying the conversation so much. Even when we encountered issues, the National Olympic Committees were willing to talk through the problems and we could find a solution.

'In terms of memories that still make me emotional? I was and still am disappointed the Vanuatu Beach Volleyball team and Sisilia (Fiji Judoka) didn't qualify for the Games as I think they are exceptional role models and set an example as to what is possible not only for women and sport in the region but the overall potential of all athletes in Oceania if given the right support and preparation. I was thrilled when Anolyn Lulu (table tennis, Vanuatu) qualified for London as she is an extraordinary person and athlete, and one of Vanuatu's first STOP HIV Champions and Kicking AIDS Out trainers, who is now the Vanuatu STOP HIV National Coordinator. I worked very closely with her and was constantly inspired by her ability to motivate and inspire others.

'Lastly, a very sad time for all of those close to Ronald Talasasa, Solomon Islands, was when his mother passed away right before the Opening Ceremony. I am still in awe of his commitment to the National Olympic Committee of the Solomon Islands and the team, to remain with them until the end of the Games and to witness the support provided from all the other members of the Pacific family at such a difficult time.

'A couple of memories make me smile. I watched Nat Cook from Australia play her last Beach Volleyball match in London. I was with Natanya Potoi and Hanisi Visanti from ONOC which, given Nat's involvement in the ONOC Athlete Commission, was great to be cheering her on together with them. We were all amazed by her ability to keep smiling and enjoy the competition despite being disappointed. Being her 5th Olympic Games she deservedly received a standing ovation.

'I also smile thinking about the crowd being swept along in their support for the Oceania weightlifters. Whether it was the charismatic performance of Manuel Minginfel or the graciousness of Ele Opelage and Itte Detanamo, all the lifters shared a little piece of what makes the Pacific unique, and represented their countries with such warmth and pride even when competing at the top of the world. The crowd adored them.

'Her Majesty the Queen and the Duke of Edinburgh visited the Olympic Village and had the good fortune of meeting athletes from Australia, New Zealand, Papua New Guinea, Nauru and the Solomon Islands. This was a very special occasion for all the athletes and Chefs de Mission involved. Having introduced a number of the National Olympic Committees to Princess Anne in 2011 during the Chefs de Mission meeting in London, to then meet the Queen a year later was certainly an extraordinary series of events. I recall Ronald Talasasa (Solomon Islands) and Ted Rutun (Federated States of Micronesia) not wanting to wash their hands after greeting Princess Anne and then after meeting the Queen the following year, Ronald stating that, "last year meeting Princess Anne was the highlight, but now, this is the best, I could die tomorrow."

'A few particular memories stick in my mind and hopefully give a flavour of why it was such a privilege to work with Oceania. From the start of my job with LOCOG, it was evident that Oceania was special as I was able to hold "meetings" and find each and every National Olympic Committee at the "Coconut corner" of the bar in Mexico during the Association of National Olympic Committees General Assembly while my colleagues tried to track down their countries and schedule meetings. My existing links with the North West and The Reporters' Academy developed during my time working at ONOC were particularly valuable as it helped to ensure that although operating in the UK we were able to mirror the collective approach of ONOC.

Sisi pointing out her small Island in the middle of the Pacific Ocean, raising awareness of her country and being a positive role model to young people and women of the Pacific.

We all worked very closely together, particularly when the International Olympic Committee Oceania Forum was held in London in December 2011, bringing sixteen NOC representatives to London to assist with preparation and then visit training-camp venues in the North West. ONOC had the foresight to ensure that these representatives were the same people that would conduct the Pre-Delegation Registration Meetings in April 2012 and then the Delegation Registration Meetings on arrival to the Olympic Village during the Games.

'I would like to thank James Macleod, Head of National Olympic Committees and National Paralympic Committees Relations for London 2012, as not only did he lead an exceptional team but his patience for Oceania and trust in my relationship with the National Olympic Committees of Oceania allowed us all to deliver a truly fantastic Games and make adjustments applicable for the region when needed. I'd also like to acknowledge Robert Vergouw who worked with me as the Oceania Regional Coordinator and is now working as the Oceania Manager for the Glasgow Commonwealth Games.

'Unfortunately, there are no Olympic medals awarded for contribution to the Olympic movement. Oceania contributes to and excels in the Olympic movement, espousing the Olympic values of friendship, excellence and respect. If I had the honour ever to present such a medal, it would be gold to the green ring of the movement.

'I would also make a special mention to the Sport Development Officers such as Siniva (Cook Islands), Dengue (Samoa), James (Vanuatu) and Andrew (Papua New Guinea) who are an asset to their National Olympic Committee and worked extremely hard in both the lead-up and during the Games. It's certainly encouraging for the region to see the next generation display such competence.

'Thank you to everyone who made the last six years such an incredible journey both personally and professionally. I look forward to seeing you again soon.'

Reflections in the Pacific

Jo Ferris, formerly Oceania Regional Manager for LOCOG, Rob Young, former North West 2012 Coordinator for London 2012 and Rob Vergouw, National Olympic Committee Regional Coordinator.

Tʜe North West Development Agency was the government-sponsored body responsible for economic development in the north-west of England, including Greater Manchester, Lancashire and Cumbria. In November 2008, almost four years before the Olympics were to be held in London, the Agency signed a partnership agreement with the Oceania National Olympic Committees (ONOC) to develop links for the period up to and including the London Games. Fundamentally the Memorandum of Understanding was all about providing training facilities for the Oceania athletes to use in their preparations for London.

Two people in particular were fundamental to this process: on behalf of ONOC their president, Dr Robin Mitchell; and on behalf of the North West Development Agency and partners across the region, Rob Young, who was the North West Co-ordinator for the London 2012 Games, based at the North West Development Agency until its closure early in 2012.

Dr Mitchell is a former Fiji National representative in athletics and hockey who by profession is a family medical practitioner. He was also national hockey coach for Fiji for six years in the 1980s while being the Fiji team physician at the Olympic Games, Commonwealth Games and Pacific Games between 1984 and 1992. Dr Mitchell has the hugely prestigious role of IOC member. Rob was part of the London 2012 Nations and Regions team within the London Organising Committee and had a role to help ensure that the region benefited from the Games. A big part of this was the Pre-Games Training Camp programme. Rob was centrally involved in helping to secure the initial agreement from ONOC and coordinating with consortia across the region who delivered the training camps. Together they are able to provide unique insights into how the Oceania–North West partnership was formed, what it achieved, and what it could possibly lead to in the future.

At first sight it might appear incongruous to think of inviting Oceania athletes to train in the damp, chilly atmosphere of England's North West. Acclimatisation for a summer of Olympic sport in London would prove to be one major benefit of making the journey from sub-tropical islands such as Nuaru or Fiji to train in the wet, wind and (occasionally) snow of Lancashire, but the many differences of culture, language, society and economy between the two regions are little short of astonishing. The total combined population of the islands that made up the unified Oceania Olympic team is around 10 million; the population of the North West is around 7 million. Then there are the wide disparities of population density, including the vast oceanic distances between island communities compared with the congestion of, say, Liverpool or Manchester; or the wide differences in terms of educational and healthcare opportunities available to the respective populations; or the fundamentally different economic profiles and cultural experiences; or, finally, the relative lack of sophisticated training facilities or coaching to be found on the Islands. And this proved to be one major reason for the links to be forged.

Rob Young explains the decision-making process from the perspective of the London Organising Committee:

The link can be seen as going back as far as the Commonwealth Games in 2002 held in Manchester. Then, all of the Oceania Commonwealth countries were involved, and it made the region seem more familiar to them. With some work in May 2008 with the World Academy of Sport we identified the opportunity to work with Oceania as a cluster, as opposed to other agreements that would be just with one country. We presented the London 2012 training camps guide in Beijing, discussing the options. The small countries would benefit from economies of scale by working together, and we saw the potential to work with the region in the future, working up to Glasgow 2014 and beyond. Not only was the agreement one of the most innovative, it was also one of the first to be signed, with it being confirmed in November 2008.

Dr Robin Mitchell explains how it all came about, from the point of view of the Pacific.

In the lead-up to the Beijing Olympics we were in discussions with several regions including the North West and Kent. However, the North West offered exactly what we wanted as a group of island nations. The North West is an iconic sporting area, which along with a programme that was more than just sport, it seemed a good fit. The people in the region were keen to work with Oceania, and looked to develop links with the communities and small towns, along with a view to continue the partnership past London 2012. The North West is in a perfect geographical location for this, being in between London and Glasgow, along with good connections to Europe, for it to be used as a European base.

Dr Mitchell outlines the aims as far as his organisation was concerned:

Generally the aims were to provide a training centre for the athletes leading up to London 2012 and beyond. Outside the sporting field, what was strong was the educational programmes, with cultural exchange and youth participation – for example the links with The Reporters' Academy. The aims developed as the period went along, and we let the countries decide specifically what they wanted, with ONOC acting in more of a facilitating role with the individual countries speaking directly with organisations in the North West.

The memorandum was not a one-sided agreement, with the North West looking to benefit from the opportunity socially, economically and through sport development for the region, along with providing the best they could for the athletes from the Pacific region.

It was not just about medals; it was about improving sporting performance and helping more athletes qualify. We aspired to develop long-term links to help develop sport in Oceania, giving more skills to athletes and coaches to improve the infrastructure in their home countries. This agreement wasn't about gaining economic benefits for the North West, but more about developing community links and benefits. The athletes' integration within the region was deep. As there were only a small number of athletes, they could work with local clubs – this gave them a good social network, providing a supporting atmosphere. This was particularly important as many of the athletes would be coming along on their own, without the support of coaches or even fellow athletes in many cases, and as such it provided a good environment to help them settle in and avoid homesickness, which ultimately ends up benefiting sporting performance.

This remarkable and broad-ranging project was marked by a great number of successes, as Rob Young explains:

For me, it was the feeling that we delivered. The fact that the agreement was for London 2012 yet discussions are under way to take these relationships forward shows that it was valued so much and is concrete proof that it has worked well. Some particular successes that stand out in my mind were seeing coaches that worked with the athletes during the camps going on to work at the Olympic Games – for example seeing Roy Wood supporting Guam wrestling, as well as Mike Liptrot supporting judo. Another success was seeing The Reporters' Academy gaining media accreditation at the Games.

From the point of view of the Pacific islands, Dr Mitchell explains what he perceives to have been the successes:

A big success was being able to secure funding and get the athletes over to England in the first place – this was a major achievement. We sparked off development of sports in the North West. For example, with Crewe seeing a new beach volleyball court being built. We have also seen the beginning of the Sports Education Programme where local universities from the North West work with the Oceania countries. We exceeded expectations in several areas, but particularly with sporting performance. We saw countries less renowned for their sporting performances, for example Nauru and Kiribati, who narrowly lost out to the sporting great of Australia.

On a similar note, he explains how the agreement has directly benefited the Pacific island nations.

We see the benefit in that the athletes who took part in the training camps performed at a higher level than ever before, plus we had higher numbers of athletes taking part. This was down to having the extra expertise and longer preparation – this clearly shows that the North West clearly helped to get the best from the athletes.

Rob takes a view towards how it has benefited in other ways, looking at the benefits to the communities in the North West.

If you take it down to a personal level, one project that stands out is The Reporters' Academy. Many saw the Olympics as something that would be good to get involved in, and the partnership with ONOC developed a link allowing the reporters to get accreditation to the Games. Another benefit was life-long friendship links that were created – these were things that were never in the memorandum, but which will not be forgotten in a hurry. You could meet these people again in 20 years' time and still relive the memories.

On the topic of memories, Rob is clear:

There were loads of memories! A particularly prominent memory was the Oceania General Assembly in 2009, a really big 'do' with the likes of Sebastian Coe and Jacques Rogge in attendance. It was a really formal dinner, yet everyone was so friendly. I sat back and thought that if you could bring this sort of atmosphere everywhere then everyone would love it. On another level, there were other memories that just seem so unusual – like boxers from Nauru taking over a judo facility and training with judo players in Kendal and getting involved with sparring practice with local players. Or the fact that Manchester Metropolitan University, based in Crewe, stepped up and built a beach volleyball court, which has resulted in the university having a beach volleyball team and other local clubs established.

For Dr Mitchell the memories are equally striking.

Seeing the young reporters in the Cook Islands was when the reality of the partnership started to come through, then when the likes of Rob Young from the North West came to meetings in the Pacific. They were part of the ONOC General Assembly since 2008, and I enjoyed seeing them becoming a bigger part of the meetings and even getting up and dancing! The Reporters' Academy also helped in bringing the games to the Pacific, and I enjoyed seeing them at the games, reading the stories and watching the films they made. We set up free-to-air TV in the countries where previously it hadn't existed, and were even able to broadcast The Reporters' Academy's films via the satellite link.

The four years proved to be a profound learning experience for the pair, with both gaining a great deal from it. Rob explained just how much he had learnt.

I learnt a heck of a lot – most importantly you need to do your homework. We did, but it was still a whole lot harder than we could ever have imagined. However, by doing our homework we managed to build up decent relationships and take on lots of opportunities of mutual help – this help was not just in delivering programmes but helped to create a spirit of working together.

The sheer scale of the partnership helped Robin to learn a lot personally:

Working with a diverse group on our side meant that we really had to keep on pushing, with the constant task of administrating everything, ensuring the best for the athletes. It worked well and I was really proud that was happening, and it was great to see the athletes being able to take part.

Many hours were spent in preparation, training, coaching and acclimatisation, but eventually the time came for the Olympic Games to begin, an incredible time for all. Rob feels able to summarise his experience of the Games quite succinctly:

The games flew by like a whirlwind. They were an amazing success, and I had to pinch myself to believe that I was a part of it. However, the scale of how amazing it was will take a really long while to sink in.

Dr Mitchell on the other hand had more of an observer's role:

The Games in London was a great Olympics. I managed to do a lot of things apart from being at the sport, so for example being part of the crowds at places like Hyde Park was really magical.

'The games flew by like a whirlwind. I had to pinch myself to believe that I was a part of it.'

From the outset it was hoped and anticipated that cooperation between the two regions might continue beyond the primary objective of London 2012, and on towards the Commonwealth Games to be held in Glasgow in 2014. There have been setbacks, not least when the British government decided to abolish the NWDA in March 2012. Despite this, both men are optimistic. As Dr Mitchell put it:

> We don't have an overall body to sign a new memorandum with, as it's tough without the North West Development Agency in place. It is a case of looking for different people, with The Reporters' Academy and universities being examples of someone holding the link together. We would like to keep the North West as a European base for preparing and competing in Europe.

From the British perspective, Rob Young is equally keen to continue cooperation:

> We are trying to get the core things in place to allow the North West to be their European training base. We are also looking at other ways in which we can help, in ways like Ian Irwin going out to Nauru to help develop boxing over there.

Determination and commitment such as this might well help secure a continuation of the strong bonds that have been forged. Some of the Islands have chosen to specialise in particular sports, another sign of continued development and increasing awareness of what is required of athletes on the biggest stages. Thus, Fiji and Papua New Guinea are looking in particular to develop athletics, while Kiribati and Nauru are focusing on boxing. Fiji, the Solomon Islands and Palau are developing judo, while the beach volleyball team, who are going from strength to strength, remain, quite naturally, the focus of Vanuatu. Fiji, Palau and American Samoa are looking to develop swimming, while other countries who were only able to join the training programme relatively close to London 2012, but who witnessed how successful those programmes could be, are seeking to use the North West more in the future.

It is clear that the legacy of London 2012 is alive and kicking, and will be a major factor in the lead-up to Glasgow 2014 and the 2016 Olympics in Rio de Janeiro. With so many willing partners on the Pacific islands and in the North West, the sporting and wider benefits are set to expand and grow from that initial memorandum of understanding that was signed in 2008.

'Where youth produced': Gemma Martin's journey

The Reporters' Academy team from Manchester on the Oceania pontoon: Matt Bowcott, Emma Cullen, Glyn McGuire, Katy Atkinson, Emma Martin and Lewis Woods.

I N   O N E   S E N S E the Olympic Games is all about dreams: the dreams of a nation, the dreams of the athletes, and the dreams of their families. And bringing such dreams a little closer to the youth of the world was absolutely central to the bidding process for the London 2012 Olympic and Paralympic Games. The London Organising Committee, led by double Olympic champion Lord Sebastian Coe, had ambitious plans to place youth at the centre of the Games, their vision famously encapsulated by their desire to 'inspire a generation'. A lasting legacy of youthful involvement in Britain and around the world was to be the crucial test of whether or not the Games had been a success.

Elevated ambitions such as these could well have led to apathy, anti-climax or ambivalence. How would the citizens of the host nation react to the news that London would indeed be hosting the 2012 Games? Would the organisers' ambitions really inspire the youth of the world, here in Britain as well as in far-removed communities such as Fiji, Papua New Guinea or the Solomon Islands? The sheer magnitude of the Games meant that it would be hard to ignore. Inevitably some people would be sceptical, perhaps cynical. For others it would be little more than a two-week event to enjoy on television. Yet, for many others, the challenge and the chance to participate would be embraced enthusiastically from day one. Surely this would be an opportunity to create a lasting legacy, to change people's lives, to make a difference. This was London's vision for the Games, and it was a vision designed to appeal not only to athletes but to a wide range of other groups in society, including volunteers, sports organisers, and many others, including aspiring journalists.

Thus began my involvement. In September 2007, just over two years after Lord Coe and his team had successfully secured the Games for London, I and Matt Bowcott were going about our everyday activities. These activities were pretty much the same as those for most 13-year-olds around the world: schooldays and 'free' weekends, sport, homework, technology, and friends. Matt and I live in Manchester, one of Britain's largest cities, around 300 km north of London and home to a diverse, multi-ethnic population of around 2 million people (if you include the surrounding suburbs). Manchester has a fine sporting heritage, including Manchester United and Manchester City football clubs, Lancashire County Cricket

Crew member Ryan interviewing the Vanuatu Beach Volleyball girls after their match at the London 2012 test event, at Horse guards parade. The film produced by the crew from the event was later showcased to Her Majesty the Queen

OCEANIA: AN ODYSSEY

Upper Crew members Lewis, Gemma, Emma and Matt receiving some valuable advice from Matai, a news journalist from the Pacific islands.

Emma and Connor interview Fijian Sisi at UCLan in Preston, where Sisi was having a medical screening and a biomechanical analysis. This sports-science aid is extended to the Pacific athletes, as part of the support provided by the North West training camps.

Club at Old Trafford, and the home of British Cycling at the Manchester Velodrome. Manchester was also proud host to the 2002 Commonwealth Games.

In many ways Matt was a typical teenager, wanting to discover and explore most things and with a keen interest in sport, enjoying Formula One and football. I must admit that, before becoming involved with the Olympics I could not really describe myself as a sports fanatic, although I did admit to 'quite liking gymnastics and dance'. This would present one challenge to London 2012's legacy vision – how can you engage young people through sport over a number of years?

Matt and I became involved with sports journalists and the Olympics following an invitation from our schools to join a voluntary programme, the aim of which was simple: to create something that could make a difference to the lives of young people over the long term, through 'money can't buy opportunities' such as working alongside professional broadcasters at some of the world's foremost sporting events.

Enter, The Reporters' Academy, a unique, not-for-profit, sports media production company which is run by, and for, young people, with the aim of helping the young people gain employment and progress in education. All organisations have aims: the message from The Reporters' Academy to the young people was 'aim higher'. Many of us were inspired by this and by London's successful bid for the Olympic and Paralympic Games.

Many young people snatched this amazing once-in-a-lifetime opportunity, and a remarkable few years were sparked off, for not only Matt and me, but a number of other young people who also embraced the opportunity to 'give it a go'. As part of the Reporter's Academy activities, the teenagers involved have produced and written radio, television and online content by attending sporting events and then having it distributed across the world.

From the outset the group decided they would go to the Olympic Games to report as official media. This would be no small task. You can't just apply for the best press seats in the house. The Reporters' Academy would need to be considered for accreditation alongside the other sports journalists of the world. Therefore, there was a process of training, then production of a high quality over a consistent period of two years in order to even have a chance of being considered. The Reporters' Academy had become the first youth organisation to attend an Olympics Games as accredited journalists.

My reaction was: 'Initially being told that we, the young reporters of The Reporters' Academy, were going to work toward getting official accreditation for the 2012 Olympic Games, well, … it seemed like a dream, and each reporter including myself wished, yet doubted that this would be possible.'

In every aspect of life, anything built to last requires solid foundations. Step by step, and making sure that everything was solid and sustainable, The Reporters' Academy began to build their 'dream house'. Key to working well in the future were initial training, breaking down confidence barriers, developing working relationships, becoming comfortable with staying away from home, and being able to work to deadlines. These were just a few of the things that were new to the youngsters, all before learning many new skills in media production.

Before long this newly created family was slowly making the dream a reality. We attended and reported on the Paralympic World Cup, the World Track Cycling Championships, Manchester United games, and even football cup finals from Wembley Stadium. This prepared the young people for being part of the media at large sporting events. Along the way, that question of 'how do you engage young people in a sporting legacy?' was never far away from the forefront of planning. Like me, not all young people have a passion for sport or the media.

The premise was simple – everyone wants to see the value of giving up their time, and everyone loves an interesting story. The first value that had to be established was the idea that young people had to be encouraged and allowed to progress and to improve themselves. They had to have 'buy in', so that they could see that The Reporters' Academy could make a real difference to their future. In addition to the skills they were learning, therefore, there was a 'wrap around' education and training programme, including opportunities for real-life work experience, interview practice, or support with writing your CV. Second, an interesting story is often one which informs you of something new, an insight into a world you would not otherwise see. Therefore, while mainstream media outlets on the whole concentrated on the sporting stories – of who won, and how the goals were scored – The Reporters' Academy sought to relate the human, social and cultural stories that lay behind, and were associated with, the athletes and sportspeople.

At an early age we were being exposed to a world that we had not experienced before:

OCEANIA: AN ODYSSEY

We covered lots of sports and situations that were new to us. We were dealing directly with adults. At each event we covered a range of stories which were broadcast on different media platforms, including the BBC and ABC in Australia, giving each reporter the opportunity of getting their name known in the media industry.

A throw-away line at the signing of the Memorandum of Understanding unwittingly provided the next watershed moment for these young people who were fast becoming well known around the sporting media circuit. As part of an interview which the reporters were carrying out, they were almost casually invited to cover the 2009 Pacific Mini Games in the Cook Islands. Four months later, and much to everyone's surprise, the official invitation arrived.

A small team of eight young people with a variety of skills was put together. Ryan Alleyne, who has a passion for editing video, Dan O'Hara the groups 'go to' person for technical expertise and advice, Peter Fry and Shane Gibb who worked well together on interviewing, the latter with a vast sporting knowledge. Emma Cullen a very good athlete herself who has a thirst for uncovering a unique story, Lewis Woods a quiet dedicated member of the team who brought great production ideas as well as a wicked sense of humour. Then there was Matt who by now had decided that a media career may be for him and so immersed himself in all aspects of production everyday. Lead by Katy and Glyn, our group leaders, the brains behind the operation. We also were lucky enough to have professional mentors Michelle and Margaret guiding us. I was lucky enough to be part of the team:

During these Games we produced various packages from different story angles, some solely focusing on the sporting events, others showing the fantastic, different cultures of the Oceania nations. This was an eye-opening opportunity, and is where my Olympic journey began. The best part of this opportunity for me was the great access we had to every media area, to share the culture and the fact that we were able to stay with the teams and build great relations that even last to this day. This event was definitely a milestone.

While on the Cook Islands I was introduced to a girl of the same age called Brianna Ricci, who was at the Pacific Mini Games along with her family who were part of the delivery team. Brianna was invited to join the young media team from the UK and to produce content during the three weeks. So began our lasting friendship between two young people from the far edges of the world but also a lasting working relationship. Brianna and I have become firm friends. It was destined to become a link-up between two great sporting cities Manchester and Melbourne (Brianna's home city). In many ways it mirrored what the Olympic and Pacific Mini Games are about: bringing young people together in the spirit of friendship.

Brianna was inspired to immerse herself in more of this activity and to open it up to more young people back home. Thus, in 2011, the Melbourne base of The Reporters' Academy was launched. With Brianna heading things up, more than ten schools have been involved in activities around sporting and cultural events.

The main purpose of the Memorandum of Understanding between Oceania and the North West was to establish North West Pre-Games

Crew member Lewis and TRA founder Glyn interviewing Giordan Harris (RMI) in front of London's iconic landmark, Tower Bridge. This is said to be Giordan's favourite photograph. Lewis was assigned accreditation to the Marshall Islands' team and built up a close relationship with the entire delegation.

Crew in the heart of the action at London 2012, reporting from the same press benches as the world's media. The crew took their responsibilities working for ONOC extremely seriously. Every day they produced film, radio programmes and press releases to tell the world about the Pacific island athletes.

Training Camps in which all of the Olympic teams from Oceania would be able to train in the north-west of England in the months leading up to the London Games. The Reporters' Academy was tasked with providing all the coverage of these training camps, including the cultural and social stories that came from these small nations of Oceania. This opportunity again allowed the young reporters to build on pre-existing relationships that would help them on their way to reporting at the Olympics.

By early 2012 the quality of the work that we at The Reporters' Academy were producing, along with the trust and mutual respect was evident. For these young people, the Olympics, Oceania's

athletes and their stories would be giving tangible substance to the idea of 'inspiring a generation'. Just a few short years after my moment of 'doubt' came the news that I would be the accredited journalist at London 2012 for the Pacific island of Palau. Three other young people from The Reporters' Academy had been entrusted with such an honour. Emma for Vanuatu, Lewis for the Marshall Islands and Matt with Tuvalu and American Samoa. Our dream of reporting at London 2012 was within touching distance. This was an incredible moment. Not only that, but my great friend Brianna would be bringing a team from Melbourne to London. Indeed, a dream come true. Yet, even at that exciting moment, it didn't feel quite as if we were achieving a dream; somehow, it just felt 'natural'. We young reporters had shared so much of the journey, and been inspired by the Pacific athletes and teams, that we all simply wanted to see that journey through, so that we could tell the world something of the Oceania islanders' story.

The way it was organised was that each reporter was assigned a country, with which they had the exciting and challenging task of being their official media representative. This enabled daily coverage of their team's Olympic journey to be publicised so that people back on the islands had an easy way to follow their country's progress.

Looking back, I often reflect on the benefits I gained from the experience.

One of the highlights of London 2012 for me was being able to get to know each athlete

while reporting and being part of their Olympic Journey, through both highs and lows. Also, being able to see the determination in the young athletes to be the best and overcome anything that stands in their way.

Eighteen-year-old Emma Cullen was The Reporters' Academy media representative for Vanuatu. She said, 'to be a media representative was a great honour, and I loved meeting people and the responsibility, it enhanced my own independence and, more importantly, my initiative.'

Of his experience, meanwhile, Matt Bowcott spoke:

Being a media representative for Tuvalu and American Samoa was an incredible experience; I took so much away from being their representative and I will always put into practice what I have got out of my Olympic

Members of the Melbourne Reporters' Academy working hard on the pontoon at St Katharine Docks during London 2012. The Reporters' Academy provided worldwide coverage of the Pacific islands teams throughout the Games, via television, radio, newspapers and websites.

moments. One of the highlights for me during my Olympic journey was seeing the athletes from my teams compete, getting the chance to see Olympians compete and then create press releases about them was a great highlight. Similarly, seeing the ceremonies and how the athletes enjoyed them added to my experience. Sitting in the Olympic Stadium watching the Opening and Closing Ceremonies will be a memory that not one of us will ever forget. The atmosphere as the national anthem was being sung is something I will always remember and the noise as Great Britain came into the stadium was phenomenal.

Despite all these highlights the young reporters also experienced some challenges, as Matt explained: 'Some of the challenges I faced included learning about the cultures of the athletes and teams as well as communicating to the teams about the stories we wanted to create and the best ways for us to do that. Such challenges only reinforced the determination of the young people to do the best job they possibly could. My opinion is that

> The Reporters' Academy has helped so many young people to grow and progress as people. Through being part of The Reporters' Academy since the age of thirteen has boosted my confidence which has enabled me to give speeches that before would have seemed impossible. Each reporter is now able to write stories on different sporting events, improving both their sports knowledge and their writing ability. Covering different angles at different events also enables us to write with a target audience in mind. This will help to fulfil the

aim of The Reporters' Academy to help young people continue on to further education or to gain employment. Many of the young people who have worked hard to snatch the opportunities given to them are now either hoping to go to, or are already at university, or in employment with various media companies including the BBC.

… The Reporters' Academy is important to young people as it shows them that they can do anything they put their minds to, just like getting to the Olympics. To any young person who wants to aspire to do great things I would say, let nothing hold you back, always try your best as nobody, not even yourself, can ask for more. If you try your best you can achieve anything you want to. Look at me. I've had these amazing opportunities that have helped me grow and I am now trying to inspire others to do the same.

Through a range of inspirational moments and aspirational activity all the hard work has paid off. That very first aim of The Reporters' Academy – to inspire young people through sport and leave a legacy inspired by London 2012 – has been achieved.

Young people at opposite ends of the world have responded to Lord Coe's speech in Singapore by becoming part of a generation inspired by the Games. I feel that along the way, perhaps they have, in some small way, changed the perception of young people today. These reporters could give their time freely, relate to adults and produce meaningful outcomes in their communities. In fact, their very own motto was made for them: The Reporters' Academy is a place 'where youth produce'.

List of Oceania athletes competing at London 2012

Women's 100 m, Preliminaries
Mihter Wendolin (FSM)
Kaingaue David (KIR)
Janice Alatoa (VAN)
Asenate Manoa (TUV)
Rubie Joy Gabriel (PLW)
Pauline Kwalea (SOL)
Patricia Taea (COK)
Toea Wisil (PNG)

Women's 100 m, Round 1
Toea Wisil (PNG)

Women's 400 m, Round 1
Danielle Alakija (FIJ)

Women's 800 m, Round 1
Amy Atkinson (GUM)
Haley Nemra (MHL)

Women's Shotput
Ana Pouhila (TGA)

Canoe/Kayak

Women's K1 Canoe Slalom	Ella Nicholas (COK)
Men's C1 1000 m	Rudolph Williams (SAM)
Men's C1 200 m	Rudolph Williams (SAM)
Men's K1 1000 m	Josh Utanga (COK)
Men's K1 200 m	Josh Utanga (COK)

Cycling: Mountain Bike

Derek Horton (GUM)

Judo

Men

−60 Kg	Tony Lomo (SOL)
−66 Kg	Raymond Ovinou (PNG)
−73 Kg	Aleni Smith (SAM)
	Sled Dowabobo (NRU)
−81 Kg	Josateki Naulu (FIJI)

−100 Kg	Anthony Liu (ASA)
+100 Kg	Nazario Fiakaifonu (VAN)
	Ricardo Blas Jr (GUM)

Women
| −63 Kg | Jennifer Anson (PLW) |

Sailing

Helema Williams (COK), Laser Radial Class

Shooting

Glenn Kable (FIJ)

Swimming

Men's 50 m Freestyle
Ching Maou Wei (ASA)

Giordan Harris (MHL)

Zachary Payne (COK)

Kerson Hadley (FSM)

Men's 100 m Freestyle
Paul Elaisa (FIJ)

Chris Duenas (GUM)

Men's 100 m Breaststroke
Amini Fonua (TGA)

Men's 100 m Butterfly
Ryan Pini (PNG)

Men's 10 km Marathon Swim
Benjamin Schulte (GUM)

Women's 50 m Freestyle
Debra Daniel (FSM)

Celeste Brown (COK)

Keesha Keane (PLW)

Ann Marie Hepler (MHL)

Judith Meauri (PNG)

Women's 100 m Freestyle
Megan Fonteno (ASA)

Women's 100 m Breaststroke
Matelita Buadromo (FIJ)
Pilar Shimizu (GUM)

Table Tennis

Yoshua Shing (VAN-male)
Anolyn Lulu (VAN-female)

Taekwondo

Male
+80 Kg   Kaino Fuataga (SAM)

Female
−49 Kg   Theresa Tona (PNG)
+67 Kg   Talitiga Crawley (SAM)

Weightlifting

Female
53 Kg   Dika Toua (PNG)
58 Kg   Jenly Wini (SOL)
63 Kg   Maria Liku (FIJ)
+75 Kg   Ele Opeloge (SAM)

Male
56 Kg   Manueli Tulo (FIJ)
62 Kg   Stevick Patris (PLW)
        Lapua Lapua (TUV)
        Manuel Minginfel (FSM)
77 Kg   Toafitu Perive (SAM)
85 Kg   Steven Kari (PNG)
94 Kg   David Katoatau (KIR)
+105 Kg   Itte Detenamo (NU)

Wrestling

Female
Freestyle 63 Kg   Maria Dunn (GUM)

Male
Greco Roman 84 Kg   Keitani Graham (FSM)
Freestyle 96 Kg   Nathaniel Tuamoheloa (ASA)